THE BABY SWIM BOOK

Cinda L. Kochen, PhD
& Janet McCabe, BA

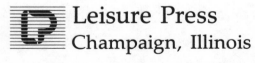

Leisure Press
Champaign, Illinois

Developmental Editor: Sue Ingels Mauck
Copy Editor: Ann Morris Bruehler
Production Director: Ernie Noa
Typesetter: Yvonne Winsor
Text Design: Julie Szamocki
Text Layout: Janet Davenport
Cover Design and Layout: Jack Davis
Printed By: Braun-Brumfield
Photographs: Page 3, © Hedda Morrison; back cover and all
              other photos by Fred M. Bonnett
Illustrations: Front cover and interior, by Alexy Pendle

ISBN: 0-88011-277-8

Library of Congress Cataloging-in-Publication Data

Kochen, Cinda L., 1947-
  The baby swim book.

  Bibliography: p.
  Includes index.
  1. Swimming for infants.   I. McCabe, Janet,
1944-   . II. Title.
GV837.25.K64   1986   797.2'1'0880542   86-10249
ISBN 0-88011-277-8

Printed in the United States of America

10 9 8 7 6 5 4 3 2 1

Leisure Press
A division of Human Kinetics Publishers, Inc.
Box 5076, Champaign, IL 61820

4-4-88 — MW-51490

In memory of our fathers
who gave much love, support, and encouragement,
Irving Lefkow and
Charles Fulton.

Contents

Acknowledgments

We wish to thank the following people for their help in making this book a reality:

Barbara Buchman, Jane Perlmutter, Lynn Reed, Judy Waller, and Lee Wright for finding obscure references.

Sigrid Bonnett, Anna Leuchs, Hal Miller, and Audrey Sheffield for translation.

Dee Coulter and Majorie Cox for manuscript suggestions.

The teachers at Janet McCabe's Swim School, especially Lynnie Middledorf.

Eric, Emily, and Molly Barron; Kevin and Linda Brown; Tami and Shane Kochen; Millard and Sue McQuaid; Mellisa, Ted, and Martha Montoya; Jennifer and Paulette Zimmerman; Emily and Robin Whitten; Zoe and Anne Cullie; Alice and Alison Burton; Patrick and Mary McCrea; Will and John McKay; Lindsey and Linda Kithil; and Casey Arnold for appearing in the photographs.

Dr. Donald L. Kellum, eye physician and surgeon; Dr. William C. Lillydahl, otorhinolaryngologist; and Dr. Richard H. Moore, pediatrician, for medical counsel.

Preface

*T*eaching your baby to swim, whether in your own home pool by yourself or in a class with other parents, can be your most memorable experience of your infant's babyhood. The physical closeness you have with your baby during swimming can be a key factor in bonding with your infant and can be the beginning of a lifelong "loving while learning" relationship. Although little research has been done on baby swimming, it indicates that swimming babies are happier and possibly healthier than their nonswimming counterparts. We personally believe this is true, although we admit we are biased having had such a delightful time teaching our own babies, as well as those enrolled in the Janet McCabe Swim School.

Though most experiences are positive ones, not every parent whose baby is involved in swimming has an equally delightful and successful time. Some babies have ended their swimming experiences in the hospital emergency room, whereas others have developed such a fear of the water they may never learn to swim.

If you want your baby to have a happy, healthful experience, you need to be informed. *The Baby Swim Book* provides you with more information on baby swimming than any other book on the subject. You will learn how water affects your baby's health, how to choose a swim school, and how to adapt the lessons to your baby's unique personality. Eight basic swimming skills are presented with clear step-by-step instructions and accompanying photographs. Typical lesson formats and helpful lesson tips are also included. Whether you are teaching your baby by yourself or in a class led by an instructor, you will learn how to teach according to your infant's psychological, physiological, and social developmental age. Moreover, you can be assured that what you learn is based on the most up-to-date research that the field of baby swimming has to offer.

For many babies at the Janet McCabe Swim School, swimming is the highlight of their babyhood. As for us, what could be more paradisiacal than frolicking in a warm water pool full of happy, babbling babies? As for you, we wish you an equally joyous time in teaching your baby to swim and hope this book makes that wish come true.

Cinda L. Kochen
Janet McCabe

1
Chapter

Benefits of Baby Swimming

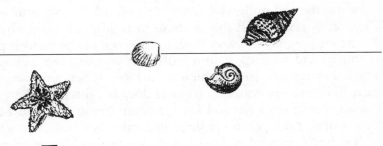

*F*or centuries, babies around the world have delighted in the water, but the phenomenon of structured baby swim classes is a recent development. Discover what to look for when choosing the best program for your baby.

Polynesian Pastimes

More than a century ago in his novel *Typee*, Herman Melville described with amazement the sight of a Polynesian mother teaching her newborn baby to swim.

One day, in company with Kory-Kory, I had repaired to the stream for the purpose of bathing, when I observed a woman sitting upon a rock in the midst of the current, and watching with the liveliest interest the gambols of something, which at first I took to be an uncommonly large species of frog that was sporting in the water near her. Attracted by the novelty of the sight, I waded towards the spot where she sat, and could hardly credit the evidence of my senses when I beheld a small infant, the period of whose birth could not have extended back

1

many days, paddling about as if it had just risen to the surface, after being hatched into existence at the bottom. Occasionally the delighted parent reached out her hands towards it, when the little thing, uttering a faint cry, and striking out its tiny limbs, would sidle for the rock, and the next moment be clasped to its mother's bosom. This was repeated again and again, the baby remaining in the stream about a minute at a time. Once or twice it made wry faces at swallowing a mouthful of water, and choked and spluttered as if on the point of strangling. At such times, however, the mother snatched it up, and by a process scarcely to be mentioned obliged it to eject the fluid. For several weeks afterwards I observed this woman bringing her child down to the stream regularly every day, in the cool of the morning and evening, and treating it to a bath. No wonder that the South Sea Islanders are so amphibious a race, when they are thus launched into the water as soon as they see the light. I am convinced that it is as natural for a human being to swim as it is for a duck. And yet in civilized communities how many able-bodied individuals die, like so many drowning kittens, from the occurrence of the most trivial accidents!

Years ago islanders, like the Typeeans, knew that swimming was good for babies. For centuries the practice flourished, and babies learned to swim almost effortlessly. Tears, screams, frantic clutches, and structured lessons were unknown to Polynesian babies. Without noticeable effort, these beautiful babies were transformed into strong swimmers, almost before learning to walk!

To most Polynesians, swimming was not a skill that had to be taught but rather an inborn ability that only required encouragement and a water environment to bring it into full bloom. Learning to swim was as much a part of growing up as walking. From the moment of birth their infants were surrounded by water and the loving hands of parents and siblings.

Western Wonders

While baby swimming reached a peak in Polynesia where the warm water provided added incentive, other cultures, particularly Californian Indians, tried to teach their babies how to

From the moment of birth their infants were surrounded by water and the loving hands of parents and siblings. Photo courtesy of Hedda Morrison.

swim. When the Yokut Indians needed to cross the swift and deep San Joaquin River, parents routinely placed their babies in baskets that were not waterproofed and pushed them across the river. Yokut mothers also used laundry time to teach their babies to swim. As one lucky Yokut child described it,

> Zac told me I could swim before I could walk. He said that my mother used to wash at the creek back of the Blankenship house. My mother would put me in the water and bend down a willow limb for me to hold. She would go on washing and leave me there for a long time. Then she taught me how to swim. I do not remember this. Zac and his mother told me about it. But I do know that I could swim as early as I can remember. (Latta, 1949, p. 228)

Despite the success of these so-called primitive cultures, it has only been in the past 20 years that western nations have discovered that baby swimming can be a marvelously civilized addition to child development programs. This idea has spread like wildfire across Australia, Germany, the Soviet Union, and the United States.

Australia

Not only do Australians live in "the land down under," but they also spend much of their time in the water. Blessed with beautiful beaches, warm water, nearly never-ending summers, and plentiful public and private pools, the Australians were among the first to recognize the benefits of teaching babies to swim.

Thanks to the Australians, who concentrated on mastering the basic baby back-floating position, we know how to train babies to get a breath before they are capable of lifting their heads. Their first efforts to perfect this position were somewhat traumatic for the babies, but these harsher drownproofing methods have given way to a gentler approach such as that popularized by Claire Timmermans. Timmermans, who traveled to the United States to study with the famed baby swim teacher Virginia Hunt Newman, opposed the drownproofing approach on the grounds that confidence is a more effective teacher than fear. In her own words, "Children who are happy and confident in the water will always be able to think themselves out of a difficult situation in it, and are thus not likely to give way to panic, with its possible tragic conclusion" (1975, p. 42).

Germany

Unlike the Australians, the Germans do not have long summers, miles of balmy beaches, and thousands of backyard pools. They swim, not because it's the obvious thing to do—most of their lakes and ocean beaches are cold—but because they find it invigoratingly healthy. To the Germans, strong bodies and minds are a natural combination.

Through their baby swim programs, Germans drew attention to the effectiveness of water play in fostering confident personalities and intellectual and physical health. In German baby classes, play is the primary mode of learning. They believe that the best learning takes place when children are allowed to make

The pool is filled with children roller skating, pushing doll buggies, and riding tricycles underwater.

their own discoveries. This is not surprising as many of the first child development specialists were German, and the first kindergarten, with its emphasis on discovery through play, was German.

German researchers have collected some impressive evidence that indicates early swimmers, when compared to both inactive children and those active in other types of play, perform better on tests measuring social, academic, motor, and personality development. The German evidence is impressive, but to impeccable researchers their results cannot be said to be proved beyond any doubt. Our personal experience tends to support the German claims; but whether the superiority of swimming babies on certain tests is actually due to swimming or to other varied reasons, such as having parents who place their children in challenging environments, is still open to debate.

Soviet Union

Weightlessness and newborns are the aspects of baby swimming the Soviets have found most fascinating. From research originating with Dr. Igor Charkovsky, many Soviet parents have concluded that newborns who spend extensive amounts of time in the water excel in a variety of areas primarily because of their adaptation to the weightless effect of water.

Beginning in the late 1960s, Charkovsky began studying the effect of swimming on babies. He became interested in baby swimming when his own infant daughter, underweight and dying, began to thrive when he started her in a swimming program. He attributed his daughter's rapid recovery to the fact that swimming, because it takes place in a weightless environment, is a particularly efficient and healthy form of exercise.

According to Charkovsky, the time to begin capitalizing on swimming's benefits is at the moment of birth. To catch this precise moment, the babies in his clinic are born in a tank of warm water while their mothers remain submerged up to their necks. At first, his ideas were laughed at and he had trouble recruiting mothers. Now, so many mothers want to volunteer, he restricts participants to the most brilliant people and the finest athletes in the Soviet population.

After their first breath above water, when the babies start to exhale, Charkovsky plunges them back underwater. Instinctively, the babies hold their breath. Almost all of their first 96 hours are spent in the tank where they eat, sleep, and swim. The advantages of such a swimming experience, at least for Charkovsky's first crop of babies who are now 12 and 13 years old, are numerous. He claims they walked earlier, matured sooner, and are now stronger, smarter, more self-confident, better looking, taller, and healthier than their peers. In one of his clinics, only 18 out of 100 swimming babies had minor colds, as compared to a control group in which 82 out of 100 nonswimming babies came down with severe colds.

Charkovsky's claims are impressive, but even under ordinary conditions, the babies in his program would be expected to be smarter and to perform better than the general population because their parents were handpicked for their above average intelligence and physical prowess. Since much of this work is classified secret and not open for inspection by foreigners, we cannot examine his data as fully as we would like. We do know that some of the babies in his program have died. We also know that researchers in other countries have been unable to totally duplicate his results with their own research, perhaps because their swimming programs are not as comprehensive and do not involve as much underwater experience.

Within the Soviet Union itself, physicians and parents are divided in their support for Charkovsky's methods. While many Soviet parents believe in the virtues of baby swimming, they, like other parents around the world, are part of a trend toward gentler methods.

United States

The back floating safety position was Australia's contribution to baby swimming. Germany drew attention to the effectiveness of water play in fostering confident personalities and intellectual and physical health. The USSR pioneered the exploration of the effects of weightlessness and submersion on newborns. The United States brought attention to the fact that swimming is very valuable in shaping a healthy emotional relationship between parent and child.

Typical of the many supporters of baby swimming in the U.S., one American physician praised it because it encouraged a lot of physical contact between mother and child. "It's like bonding again—and that's good" (Berman, 1981, p. 73). Parents often explain that they find the classes immensely pleasurable because of the enjoyable, close relationship they develop with their children.

Baby swimming first became popular in the U.S. in the late 1960s with the publication of Virginia Hunt Newman's book describing how she taught the children of Hollywood superstar Bing Crosby to swim. Love, praise, and letting each child progress at his or her own rate were the keys to her approach. About that time, the drownproofing craze burst onto the scene. Schools that claimed they could teach babies to survive alone in the water sprouted up in Arizona, California, and Florida, places where baby drownings had reached epidemic proportions. Meanwhile, schools in the gentle, loving Newman tradition continued their quiet revolution.

The drownproofing schools made local and national headlines, but because their success entailed traumatic, questionable methods, they were never officially sanctioned by the large swimming associations such as the American Red Cross, YMCA, and YWCA. Physicians, too, were reluctant to endorse the classes. Few babies were actually trained by drownproofing compared to the nurturing approach, but they got most of the media attention. As news of accidents during such classes have come to light, many parents and professionals are reaffirming their belief in the gentle approach. Americans are finally realizing that their own contribution to baby swimming—a gentle approach with emphasis on the parent-child relationship—is actually one of the best reasons for teaching babies to swim.

Good Reasons for Teaching Babies to Swim

Baby swimming can be started as soon as the circumcision has healed and the umbilical cord has fallen off. For the very young we recommend home bathtub play or newborn classes in which massage and just being in the water are the goals of the lesson. If you do decide swimming would be a valuable activity for your youngster, you will not be able to cite much research to support your decision. The experimental nature of the research and the reluctance of researchers to probe and manipulate babies make hard-nosed research a formidable task. Listed below are 13 reasons for baby swimming that our experience and some empirical data have shown to be valuable.

Teachability

1. Babies less than a year old accept the water more readily than older children. Often, they willingly go underwater the first lesson. Children older than 3 years may require eight to ten lessons before submerging their heads.
2. Fear of water is acquired as children grow older. The longer a baby is kept away from the water, the more likely the child will develop aquaphobia.

3. Human infants are adapted to swimming. When submerged, they automatically hold their breath and make swimming movements. These behaviors begin to fade, however, as early as 3 months of age.

* *Physical Development*

4. Babies can exercise more muscles in the water; they are less restricted by gravity and their inability to sit or stand. This increased strength often manifests itself in early acquisition of physical skills, like walking.
5. Swimming improves babies' cardiovascular fitness. Although babies are limited in how much they can improve their endurance, swimming does have a beneficial effect.
6. Early mastery of water movement gives children a head start in learning basic swimming skills. Stroke instruction can begin as early as age 2-1/2 years for children who have had proper preparation.
7. Water helps improve coordination and balance by forcing babies to move bilaterally to maintain their equilibrium.
8. Warm water, combined with gentle exercise, relaxes and stimulates babies' appetites. They usually sleep and eat better on swimming days.
9. Doctors often recommend swimming as the exercise of choice for asthmatics. For many asthmatics, exercise produces bronchial hyperactivity. Swimming stimulates less wheezing than other forms of exercise, possibly because the warm, moist air around pools is less irritating to the lungs.

* *Psychological Development*

10. Babies flourish in the focused attention their parents lavish on them during swimming. Parents often confess that the lessons provide the only time they can spend 30 pleasurable, uninterrupted minutes with their babies.
11. As babies learn how to maneuver in the water on their own, their independence and self-confidence blossom as evidenced by the ear-to-ear grins stretching across their faces. That independence and self-confidence may foster increased intelligence.

12. Swimming provides babies with lots of skin-to-skin contact with their parents. That, psychologists say, may deepen the bond between parent and child.
13. Learning to swim is not only a fun, healthful activity, but a safety measure as well. In the United States, drowning is the second greatest cause of accidental death in children (motor vehicle accidents are first). More than 1,760 children drown each year. All children should learn how to swim to reduce their chances of drowning and to free them from the paralyzing effects of fear and panic when near the water.

Dangerous or Safe?

Clearly, starting swimming when your baby is young has many advantages, but they are worthless if they can be attained only by risking your baby's health. Some people do not support baby swim classes, and one of the following four reasons is usually cited for their opposition:

First, opponents doubt swimming is a natural function. They explain that while it's true that babies spend their first 9 months submerged in utero, they had umbilical cords to breathe for them, instead of lungs. What was natural for babies before birth becomes unnatural after birth. That argument can be countered by the fact that it is natural for babies to hold their breath when submerged and it is natural for their bodies to automatically conserve oxygen and make swimming movements. The proof, at least for those of us who have taught babies, lies in the fact that thousands of babies have learned to swim with scarcely a whimper.

Another frequent criticism is that classes are simply a modern version of "keeping up with the Joneses." The baby who has everything must also have swimming lessons, preparing the way for the child to be best swimmer on the block. Certainly, such babies, pushed into mastering skills they are not ready for, can become frustrated, but in properly managed classes this is rarely the case.

⚹ Good teachers discourage parents from pushing their babies into frustrating situations. Instead they cultivate a relaxed, non-stressful atmosphere and present babies only with those challenges that are appropriate. Teachers with healthy attitudes realize that most of the babies in their classes will not grow up to be competitive swimmers. Not until children can consciously think about improving their strokes and not until they have passed through puberty, when hormones favor muscular growth and development of endurance, will swimming lessons have a great effect on their competitive ability. Baby swimming lessons do lead children to love the water and to early mastery of basic skills. This familiarity with the water may, in turn, lead them into swimming competition, but not necessarily.

A third major criticism of baby swimming is that the classes are dangerous and life-threatening. Infant hospitalizations in drownproofing-type classes rightfully have alarmed parents and swimming authorities. Many have overreacted by condemning all submersion. The blame should fall upon the extreme methods used in such classes and not on the mere fact the babies were submerged. Discerning parents recognize that it's not baby swimming that is harmful, but rather that certain swim schools use harmful practices. Submersion is harmless if done properly.

In addition to the above three common reasons for opposing baby swimming is a fourth but less popular one. Those with this point of view criticize most baby swimming classes, not because they are too dangerous, but rather because they are too gentle. John W. Schiefflin, MD, a leading proponent of this point of view, objects to these gentle classes because they do not stress survival. He believes they foster overconfidence and a lack of fear, which could lead to drowning.

Instead of gentle classes, Schiefflin promotes a survival program, called aquakinetics, which is a type of drownproofing. The program involves dropping fully clothed children from a height of 3 feet or more and leaving them to float alone for up to 30 minutes. Another survival technique is to push the children's feet over their heads, while in the water, so they learn how to adapt to repeated submersions.

Schiefflin is not alone in his viewpoint. Other swim schools agree with this philosophy. Nevertheless, we believe that as long as extreme drownproofing methods are used, babies in the classes run a risk of becoming water intoxicated, which can lead to death.

Because not all baby swim classes are taught by competent instructors, we do not advocate rushing out to the nearest pool and signing up for the next baby class. The benefits of baby swimming pertain only to those classes that are properly managed. If the first class you find is taught by an instructor with no training in baby swimming, or the school's philosophy emphasizes forced submersion, the lessons may be hazardous to your baby's health.

Before signing up for any baby swimming class, first check with your physician to see if your baby has a medical problem that may be aggravated by swimming. Then, visit several schools and talk to the teachers to find out their philosophy and experience. If your first impression is upsetting because the class is crowded with crying babies and distressed parents, chances are you and your baby won't be happy there either.

Keep in mind, though, that every class has an occasional off day, so crying is not always a true indicator of poor teaching. To determine if it is just an off day, observe the way the instructor and parents handle the children. Are they loving and understanding when dealing with the children's problems, or are they demanding and impatient? If they are the latter, chances are the children are always unhappy.

The drawbacks of other classes may be more subtle. Schools that have a high rate of instructor turnover usually offer baby swimming classes only because they are profitable and in demand, not because they want to teach babies. Such schools usually do not take time to develop a well-thought-out baby program or to cultivate experienced, knowledgeable teachers. They may consider baby classes as less prestigious than their advanced classes and hire beginning, inexperienced instructors to teach them. Expect to receive bad advice and poor instruction in such a school.

Another indicator that a swim school should be avoided is the condition of the pool itself. Is the water warm? Are the locker rooms clean? Do your eyes burn when you walk into the pool area? If the management says the water is kept below 82° F because the pool is used by lap swimmers who find warm water stifling, you can be fairly sure your baby will be miserably cold and crying only 10 minutes into the lesson. If your eyes become irritated in the pool air, chances are the pool is poorly maintained. All of these factors make the lessons less enjoyable.

Of course, no swim school is perfect, and even the best ones have weak spots. But if all the swimming classes near you seem to have an overwhelming number of disadvantages, you may be wiser to avoid them completely. That does not mean you have to skip baby swimming altogether. You simply will have to teach your baby yourself in the nearest available warm pool (pools affiliated with hospitals are generally warmer) or your own family bathtub. Although your child will not have the chance to learn by imitating other babies and you will miss out on socializing with other parents, you still can share an enjoyable learning experience with your baby.

To help you decide whether a swim school is good or bad, compare it to the following list.

Desirables

✝1.   Happy atmosphere: A happy, noncompetitive atmosphere is usually a good indication that your baby will be encouraged to learn in an individual way. The atmosphere should be neither chaotic nor repressive, but rather kept under control by a teacher who allows a healthy amount of spontaneity. The teacher should provide opportunities for your baby's social, intellectual, and emotional growth as well as swimming instruction.

Look for a happy atmosphere in a baby swim class.

2. Loving teachers: Look for a teacher who loves babies for what they are and not for what he or she can teach them. Because you will be working closely with the teacher, that person should be someone whose opinion you respect and with whom you can communicate easily. Much of what your baby learns during swimming lessons is dependent on the relationships between you and the teacher and your baby and the teacher.

3. Involved children: Look at the children's faces. They should be smiling and interested in what is going on. The teacher should encourage the child to initiate many of the actions.

4. Child-oriented language: Conversation during the lesson should be directed toward the children and their parents. Your baby should have lots of opportunities for eye contact during conversations with you or the teacher. Adults should respect your baby's right to talk and every effort should be made to understand what the child is trying to communicate.

5. Educationally sound program: The overall program should be based on child development principles. Using these principles to develop goals, the teacher can then individualize instruction to meet the needs of each baby in the class. As a general rule, there should be no more than eight babies per teacher. Classtime should be divided into about 25 minutes of instruction and 5 minutes of free time, with at least one lesson per week. Look for programs that offer a variety of classes for babies, based on age and ability, like special classes for newborns, handicapped babies, toddlers, beginning 2-year-olds, and advanced 2-year-olds.

6. Year-round sessions: During lapses between sessions, it's inevitable that your baby will forget some skills. The fewer water experiences your baby has had, the more likely those experiences are not well ingrained, and the easier they will be forgotten. As your baby matures, longer periods between the sessions can be tolerated without large-scale forgetting.

If you take lessons only in the summer, expect at least half of what was learned to be forgotten. Taking at least one other session helps your baby remember more. If your swim school does not offer year-round sessions, you can substitute informal swimming sessions in the bathtub.

Contrary to popular belief, winter is an excellent time to take swimming lessons. Winter swimmers who are properly dried and warmed have no more illnesses than non-swimmers. Babies learn equally well in both summer and winter classes. While you may be more in the mood to swim in the summer, winter sessions have their advantages too. They are less crowded so they may be more relaxing, and you will probably get more personal attention from the teacher. Winter classes are also more comfortable as they are held indoors where the temperature and wind can be better controlled.

Avoidables

1. Aggressive teachers: Teachers whose primary concern is to force children to comply with their teaching techniques most likely will ignore your baby's thoughts and feelings. Aggressive teachers may teach your baby to swim, but they also will teach the child that learning is a pain and teachers are ogres.

2. Forceful techniques: Schools that believe the best way to teach swimming is through repeated submersion may be hazardous to your baby's health. Babies forced to submerge repeatedly often swallow so much water they become water intoxicated, a potentially fatal condition. Force used to teach other skills, such as jumping into the water or back floating, is also unwise. Your baby may react by becoming rebellious or apathetic, resulting in the loss of the exuberance and motivation needed for the child to achieve full potential.

3. Crying babies: If babies cry throughout most of every lesson, little time is left over to learn to swim. Crying, of course, is a normal aspect of babyhood, and occasional tears are normal. When the crying becomes continuous, though, and does not vary from lesson to lesson, chances are you and your baby are the victims of poor teaching.

4. Boisterous, older children: Baby lessons are often held at the same time as those of older kids. Unless their noise and splashing are controlled, your baby may become distracted and possibly frightened. The teacher should either make sure

the older children calm down or rearrange the classes to minimize the conflict.

5. Secretive schools: Schools that are really interested in babies love to talk about their programs. They have had so many wonderful experiences, they are eager to share them with you. Some schools, however, seem to be too busy to explain their program to you. Such schools also may discourage you from observing. Avoid them.

6. Side-lined parents: Babies less than 2 years old usually are happier and learn best when their parents are nearby. But some swim schools do not allow parents to teach their own babies. Instead, parents are relegated to sitting on the sidelines. As a passive observer, you miss out on three of the main reasons for teaching your baby to swim: (a) the intensification of bonding between you and your baby; (b) the discovery that learning can be a fun, shared experience; and (c) the opportunity to tailor the classes to you and your baby's unique relationship.

7. Wild claims: Schools that claim they will drownproof your baby or teach the child to swim in less than a week should invite your suspicion. To even come close to making good on their claims, they have to use drastic, dangerous, teaching techniques. If gentle, prudent methods are used, your baby will not learn to swim in six easy lessons, nor will the child be drownproofed. Avoid being disappointed. Consider only those schools with realistic goals.

2
Chapter

The Love Factor

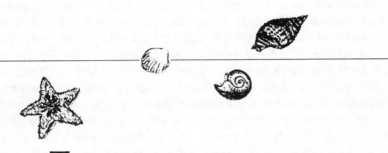

The most crucial factor in teaching your baby to swim is love. Parents often confess the lessons are a very special time in which they can devote all their attention to their baby. Whether or not the child learns to swim becomes less important as parents discover the fun and joy of playing with their baby.

Paradise or Battlefield?

On Earth, at least, the perfect paradise does not exist, but some baby swim classes come close. Babies frolic about the pool like water sprites, while their moms and dads, having forgotten the tribulations of daily life, share in their babies' joy. What a beautiful picture it is! It is so satisfying to know that there really are baby swim classes like this around the world.

Unfortunately, many other baby swim classes are battlefields. These distressful classes are crowded with frowning parents demanding that their children conquer the water. Not surprisingly, their babies usually counterattack with terrified cries. With most of the classtime consumed by crying, precious few minutes are left over to learn how to swim. The babies spend most of the lesson learning to fear the water and to distrust their parents.

Given a choice, we suspect you would prefer the relaxed, happy lesson over the stressful, discordant one. Not only would you be happier in such a class, but your baby would probably learn more and rebel less against your instruction. In relaxed classes where your baby is encouraged rather than forced to master a skill, the child has little reason to fear you, the teacher, or the water and more likely will cooperate. To recreate the paradisiacal class, you must be understanding and receptive to your child's feelings. In doing so, you open the lines of communication that can enrich your relationship with your baby.

Whether the swimming class you are enrolled in becomes a paradise or battlefield is largely up to you. Although you may have chosen a class with a happy atmosphere, you can transform the lesson into a battlefield if your goals are in the wrong order. Spending a loving, happy time with your baby should be first on your list of priorities. Teaching your baby to swim should be second. If you succeed in accomplishing the first goal, the second one will take care of itself.

Many parents who start the classes believe that teaching their babies to swim is their primary goal, but they change their priorities after the first several lessons. Rarely in their lives have parents had so many opportunities to enjoy their babies. With no phones or television to interrupt them, parents often discover for the first time just how marvelous playing with their baby can be.

Loving Tools

The word "love" is so overused that it seems rather trite. Certainly you love your baby. Loving your baby is such a natural thing that it goes without saying. While you may love your baby, many times your baby does not know that, which is why you need to focus on transmitting that love during swimming class. It's not enough to love your child; you also must communicate it. The better you communicate that love during swimming class, the more your baby will learn. There are millions of ways to show your love, but we will concentrate on four ways that are easily adapted to the water environment. They are unconditional love, eye contact, physical contact, and focused attention (Campbell, 1977).

Unconditional Love

Unconditional love forms the foundation of the relationship you have with your baby. Only love without prerequisites tacked on can insure that your child will be self-motivated to develop to his or her full swimming potential. It also protects your baby from other undermining effects the child may encounter in the water, such as fear, failure, anxiety, and insecurity. Unconditional love means loving your baby no matter what happens.

This does not mean, of course, that you must always like your child's behavior, but it does mean you should communicate your love to the child—especially when you dislike the behavior or when the child fails. No matter if your baby cannot swim to the side or back float unaided, the child still needs the security of love. In fact, it's especially after your child fails that unconditional love is most important. If you only express your love when your baby pleases you, the child will not feel genuinely loved. Instead, feelings of insecurity, incompetence, and unworthiness will fill up the void left by your withdrawal of love.

To convince your baby of your unconditional love, praise the child for attempting a task even though the task was not performed perfectly. Children who are praised only when they succeed are quick to conclude that their parents' love is for accomplishments, not the children themselves. Learning to swim then becomes something they do to please their parents. While they may continue to try, their attempts are rather joyless.

✳ Eye Contact

Eye contact, looking directly into your baby's eyes, is another easy way to express love when in the pool. In fact, eye contact is easier to use in the water than on land because you constantly have to watch your baby's face to make sure it does not accidentally drop under the water. Eye contact is a very effective way of expressing love. The more eye contact you make, the more the child feels loved, and the more lovable your baby becomes.

Eye contact is a very effective way of expressing love to your child.

The feelings your baby has about you are very much affected by whether or not you look directly at your baby. Your baby will be more inclined to feel emotionally close to you if you can maintain pleasant eye contact. The child will be assured that your love is genuine. Be careful, though, not to restrict your pleasant eye contact to those times your baby is successful. Remember genuine love is not contingent on success or failure.

Physical Contact

Physical contact, hugging and touching, is another way of communicating love. It, too, is conducive to swimming lessons where you are forced to hold your baby most of the time. Although most of us know that we can show our children we love them by hugging them, studies show that we actually avoid touching our children. Usually, we touch them only when we have to, as when diapering or dressing them. The situation is worse for boys. Boys less than a year old receive one fifth less physical affection than girls.

When in the water you are forced to have lots of physical contact with your baby. If your baby spends more than 15 seconds out of your arms, the child may choke and become frightened. This is one of those instances where you cannot have too much of a good thing. Physical contact in the water is especially gratifying because it is that special, very close, skin-to-skin contact that some researchers say is so important to bonding.

Focused Attention

Unconditional love, eye contact, and physical contact are all easy ways to shower your baby with love during swimming. Focused attention is another good way, but it is a bit more elusive. Basically, it means watching and listening to your child with complete attention. It makes your baby feel self-confident and important. Your baby becomes more aware of its abilities and is more self-motivated to exercise them.

It's easy to make excuses for not giving your baby focused attention. You are busy talking to the teacher; you are distracted by the cries of another child; you are preoccupied with planning your schedule for the rest of the day; you are mulling over the argument you had yesterday with your spouse or supervisor. To give your baby focused attention you must forget the past, not worry about the future, and concentrate on what your baby is thinking and doing in the present.

If you can do that, you send your baby the message that you feel the child is important enough to merit your uncompromising regard. The positive effects on intelligence of feeling important and influential were found by German researchers to be by-products of learning to swim. By giving your baby focused attention, you make your child feel important and competent—factors that can motivate a person to try to master more challenging skills and possibly increase intelligence.

Being in the water offers many opportunities to express your love for your child. That is why so many parents whose first priority initially is to teach their babies to swim soon change that priority to enjoying their babies. They were never before forced to use so much eye and physical contact and never had the chance to learn how wonderful it feels. Many parents express the viewpoint that their main reason for coming to class is because it gives them the chance to spend an enjoyable, intimate time with their children.

Four Approaches to Baby Swimming

Gentler classes, in which parents are encouraged to play with their babies, seem to be the wave of the future in major countries, but the present potpourri of approaches gives parents a wide variety of classes from which to choose. The four most common approaches are: drownproofing, recreational, competitive, and TLC (Tender Loving Care).

✴ *Drownproofing*

Drownproofing is known by a variety of terms including water-training, pool-proofing, and water-proofing. While the terminology may differ, all such approaches concentrate on a procedure in which babies are taught to roll over onto their backs, extend their heads, and position their faces out of the water. Typically, the classes are taught on a one-to-one basis, with the teacher directly instructing the baby. Parents are discouraged from participating and may be barred from observation. Babies usually scream during the training procedure, but their cries are purposely ignored to teach them they have no choice but to wait until help arrives. They are often left in this position for 20 to 30 minutes.

The basic philosophy of such schools is that learning to save oneself in a panic situation outweighs the benefits of feeling loved and secure in the water. Proponents claim the traumatizing effect the procedure has on babies is short-lived and that the children learn to love the water. More important, the teachers in such classes say such training has saved lives.

After the babies in these classes master back floating (not all of them can), the disorientation phase begins, its purpose being to rehearse the frightening effects of an actual drowning. The babies, often fully clothed, may be thrown into the water from a height of several feet or pulled underwater and rotated in several directions. The baby is allowed to flounder until surfacing in the drownproofing position.

Drownproofing methods have always been criticized. The harsh techniques simply do not fit with current child development theories that emphasize love and trust. Some schools boast that they monitor the babies' vital signs and have emergency equipment readily available should a problem arise, but many parents find such reassurances hollow. Understandably, they do not want to enroll their babies in any class that is even remotely life threatening.

As far as the main justification for such classes—drowning prevention—recent evidence points in the other direction. Cases of drownproofed babies who drown, and babies in the classes who become water intoxicated, may outnumber those babies who have saved themselves because they were drownproofed.

No one can guarantee that a baby is drownproofed. The actual conditions surrounding an accident are certain to confuse the baby, despite disorientation practice. The water may be colder or rougher; the child may have been injured in the fall or may panic knowing the teacher and parent are not lurking on the sidelines. Drownproofing has not prevented a significant number of drownings, but watchful attentive parents have. One popular criticism of drownproofing warns that parents, lulled into thinking their baby is safe near the water, grow lax in their supervision and are actually inviting an accident to happen.

Opponents question why it's necessary to traumatize a baby to prepare the child for a situation (drowning) that is unlikely to occur. Preparing a baby for the worst, before the child has learned to cope with everyday life, may be asking too much. Some psychologists believe the techniques are cruel and may afflict the child with lifelong emotional damage. As for the claims that learning to save themselves makes babies feel confident, the terminology is misleading. Instead, they must wait passively for an adult to come to the rescue. The fear of being abandoned may be more acute to the baby than the fear of drowning. Situations that force people to wait passively, not knowing their fate, increase tension and can cause psychosomatic illnesses in mature adults. What happens to babies in the same situation is not known, but it is doubtful the outcome is rosy.

Drownproofed babies may also have a difficult time learning to swim prone when they become older. During drownproofing they are forced to repress their own natural instinct to swim prone. Instead, they are taught that the back position is the only way to survive in the water. Later when they are older and practicing the basic swimming strokes, they must unlearn their avoidance of the stomach position.

We believe drownproofing methods are dangerous. The CNCA (Council for National Cooperation in Aquatics, which includes such organizations as the American Red Cross) discourages such classes. The drawbacks to drownproofing are numerous and the advantages are few. Is your baby's health and psyche worth the rare possibility that the child might fall into the water when you are not around? Isn't the small amount of extra parenting required to always know where your baby is a better way of preventing drowning?

Recreational

"The water is fun! There is nothing to fear!" Teaching babies to enjoy the water is the main goal of recreational baby swim programs. The emphasis is clearly on play, and instructors strive to make the lessons positive, happy experiences. Parents are often left alone to play with their babies and do whatever pleases them. The goal is to have fun with little or no accompanying instruction.

Group games are sometimes played, but their purpose is mainly for entertainment. Toys usually crowd the pool, and occasionally complete swing sets and jungle gyms are partially submerged. Recreational classes, like TLC classes, are fun and parents and children enjoy a happy time together. The difference between the classes lies in the fact that in TLC classes, most of the games and toys are used because they assist in reinforcing certain skills, whereas in recreational classes the purpose of games is to have fun. The mere fact that babies and parents have fun together in the classes makes them worthwhile.

Competitive

Swimming clubs that place heavy emphasis on their swim teams often offer classes for babies. Rather than a place to have fun or teach water adaptation, the classes are the first step in building competitive swimmers. To maximize their babies' talents, parents and teachers in these classes often ask their children to do more than they can easily handle. The classes resemble stroke clinics where the emphasis is on the stroke rather than the child.

In competitive programs, while pressuring their children, parents, too, may feel stressed. The temptation to compare babies is hard to resist, and parents often wind up comparing their own parenting skills to determine who is producing the best child. The tension in such a situation is unhealthy for everyone.

Nor is competitive swimming at very young ages worthwhile, even for children who have natural swimming talent. Burnout is a common by-product of early competition, especially when that competition rewards only the winners. An even worse drawback is the prospect of permanent physical injury to a child's growing body. By exercising the same muscles or joints over and over to perfect a skill, a baby's immature musculature, joints, and bones may suffer irreparable damage. Simply stated, baby swimming does not have long-term ramifications for competition. Later swimming success is much more dependent on personality, body type, and willingness to train day in and day out. Developing an early love of the water during a baby class is probably more important in later competitive success than stroke refinement. For these reasons we do not recommend competitive baby swim classes.

TLC

Polynesian is the best way to describe the TLC approach. The underlying philosophy of TLC is that swimming comes very naturally to infants. It's also believed to be very important for the parents to be close by for praise and encouragement. Parents are instructed to put the emphasis on helping their babies master the water on their own, so that their babies develop true self-confidence.

TLC babies do face demands, however. Just as the Polynesians allow their babies to flounder momentarily to regain their balance, parents in TLC classes keep nudging their babies to attempt more difficult skills. At first, it's not obvious that the babies are being challenged, because the pressure is so low key, but over a series of 30 to 40 lessons the babies emerge knowing how to swim.

Another basic tenet of TLC philosophy is that learning to swim is accomplished more easily and quickly when babies are happy, secure, and with the most meaningful person in their lives, usually Mom or Dad. Teachers do not directly handle each baby, as in drownproofing. Instead, the teachers, keeping a low profile, advise the parents as to what to do throughout the lesson. The basic instructional unit is the parent/child pair.

Skills are introduced gradually and never forced on crying babies. Praise, hugs, kisses, and past accomplishments are all the motivation most babies need to attempt new skills. Happy, confident babies are the rule. Babies are encouraged to learn underwater skills, but only at a relaxed, enjoyable rate.

The babies are never dropped from a height into the water, nor are they forced to submerge. They also learn skills that form the foundation for later, more formal swimming instruction. Games are common diversions as with the recreational method, but they are played to reinforce new skills as well as for entertainment. Each class ends with free time, giving the babies a chance to do whatever they wish.

The TLC method is the one taught in chapter 6.

3
Chapter

Undercurrents: Your Baby's Personality and Reflexes

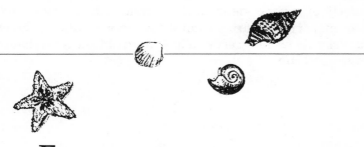

*E*ach child has a unique personality, but many of an infant's behaviors are the result of in-born reflexes. Learn how to control these reflexes and adapt lessons to your child's characteristics.

Celebrate Your Baby's Uniqueness

Guiding your baby successfully through swimming lessons is a challenge. No one can tell you exactly how to handle each situation. Your baby's intellectual, emotional, physical, and social makeup is unique. Some babies react to the water with love at first sight. Some resent giving up their warm blanket wrappings for the bareness of a swimsuit. Some have a high proportion of fatty tissue and float easily, while others have heavy bones and tend to sink.

Whether you are teaching your baby yourself or are assisted by an instructor, remember that each parent/child pair follows a unique journey. Although this book maps out the general course to follow, you will have to handle each bump and flat tire by following your own intuition. Resist comparing the route your baby takes with those of other babies. Only by concentrating on your own child's unique temperament and abilities will you be able to tailor instruction to your baby's specific needs.

While no two babies are exactly alike, during lessons most babies fall into one of the following three categories: eager, cautious, and typical. By knowing the category your baby best fits, you can often anticipate your child's responses and avoid problems. Eager babies respond rambunctiously to the water. They laugh, splash, and demand that Mom or Dad hold them loosely so they can experiment on their own. They are physically active, independent, and unafraid. Eager babies usually master motor skills earlier than their peers. To them, the water is marvelously exciting, especially if Mom or Dad gives them freedom to lead the way.

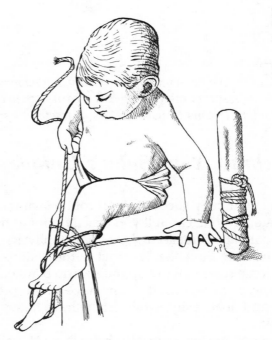

Cautious babies are suspicious of the water and cling tightly to Mom or Dad. They resist even gentle efforts to get them to explore the water environment.

Cautious babies are suspicious of the water and cling tightly to Mom or Dad. They resist even gentle efforts to get them to explore the water environment. Watching other babies play in the water does not inspire them. They attempt new skills only when they decide they are ready. Cautious babies can learn to love the water. During the first lessons, though, they need to be held closely and allowed to progress at their own plodding rate. By the time the second year of lessons rolls around, these once cautious babies may have turned into eager ones, energetic and raring to go.

Halfway between the eager and cautious babies are the typical ones. While not as fearful as the cautious babies, they are more reluctant than the eager ones to break away from Mom or Dad. Eventually, they do attempt new water skills, but only after watching their parent or another baby try a skill first. Typical babies are usually not afraid of the water, but they are not self-starters. They need encouragement and assurance to move on to more difficult skills.

By knowing your child's temperamental category, you can choose an instructional approach that complements your baby's personality. If you are not teaching your baby yourself, discuss with the teacher which category you believe best fits your child. In chapter 6, The Eight Basic Skills, separate sections explain how to adapt the lessons to eager and cautious babies. The rest of the book is geared to typical children.

In choosing your baby's temperamental category, don't assume he or she is a certain type merely because your child seems to behave that way at home. Babies often exhibit different temperaments in the water than on land. After several swimming lessons, you will be better able to judge the temperamental category your baby best fits when in the water.

Although the majority of babies maintain the same basic temperament, once you decide on a category, don't assume that fit will be permanent. As your baby matures, the youngster may switch categories. Then, you and your instructor must switch categories, too, and adapt your teaching approach to your baby's current temperament.

Channel Your Child's Fears

Aquaphobia, fear of water, is not inborn. Children learn to fear the water by watching their parents, their peers, or from their own water experience.

Most infants under 6 months of age have not had a chance to develop aquaphobia, so they usually adapt to swimming lessons fearlessly. They are used to being carried along with their parents to different places. Going to the pool with Mom or Dad is not much different from going to the grocery store. For infants this young, their worries revolve around who they are with and how well they are cared for, not where they are.

It's also easier for young infants to adapt to the water, because they have not yet had time to formulate their own attitude about swimming. For the most part, their attitude will be the same as that of their parents. As long as they are comfortable, warm, rested, fed, and held closely, they are rather nonchalant about it.

Older babies are more likely to have difficulty making an adjustment to the water. As children mature, they become accustomed to a certain set of surroundings and may become upset when introduced to unfamiliar environments. By age 2-1/2 years, changes and new experiences are often viewed as threatening. It's at this age aquaphobia may start to develop.

Starting swimming after age 2 means your child will need lots of time to experiment with the water before deciding that it's an acceptable place. Forcing your baby underwater before the child is ready will, at the least, result in tears or tantrums. At the worst, it may lead to lifelong fear of water.

If your child is over age 2, the first lessons will be spent getting adjusted to the new, wet environment. Each water skill must be introduced slowly to allow time to desensitize your baby to the water. If you were a bit adventuresome during your baby's first years and did not rush to the rescue every time your baby faced a problem, your child will probably meet the challenge of swimming confidently.

Babies who start swimming after age 2 are not the only ones who develop problems. Even if your baby started swimming under age 6 months, the child may pass through a stage around 2-1/2 years in which he or she seems frightened of the water.

Although your baby may have accepted the water without question during the first years, as your child starts to formulate opinions, he or she may need to readjust to the water from a more mature point of view. If this happens to your baby, don't belittle your child's concern. Instead, ease up on teaching the harder skills and respect your baby's worried feelings. Whatever you do, do not force underwater swimming. For a temporary time, lower your expectations to your baby's current emotional level. Fears at this age are common, but usually short-lived if handled with understanding and encouragement.

Fearful stages are a normal part of childhood, but your baby is more likely to emerge from these periods unscathed if you never use fear as a method of discipline. Never threaten your child by saying something like, "If you don't swim underwater, you can't sleep with your teddy bear tonight." It's better to handle fears by encouraging your child to express the reasons for being frightened of performing a skill. Then, you can be supportive, and, if the child is old enough, explain why there is no reason to be afraid. Follow your explanation with positive reinforcement. Pair the feared action, such as underwater swimming, with a favorite one, such as hugging a toy. Or, make a deal with your baby, such as saying, "If you jump in, I'll hold your hand." Praise your child for each step forward. Each of these little accomplishments builds confidence and eventually leads to the final defeat of fear.

Manage Your Infant's Reflexes

"You've got to be kidding!" That is probably your first reaction to the idea that your baby's reflexes can be controlled. After all, aren't reflexes simply reactions that happen spontaneously and without any conscious effort? How can a newborn's reflexive reactions be controlled? When dealing with infants, isn't the best advice just to be patient and wait out the unpleasant moments?

While it is true that you cannot stop a reflexive response once it has been stimulated, the stimulation that sets off the reaction in the first place can be controlled. Wise parents have controlled their baby's involuntary responses almost since time began. For example, parents have swaddled their newborns for centuries by wrapping them snugly in blankets so their arms and legs would not flail aimlessly. They knew that when their infants' arms and legs were loose, the babies were more likely to cry. What they did not realize was that they were controlling the Moro reflex.

When your infant is taken into a pool or given a bath, certain reflexes must be controlled or the child will cry. To prevent crying episodes with your infant, you must help the child screen out the inappropriate stimuli that stimulate them. The younger your baby, the more stimuli you will have to block. As your baby grows, many of these reflexes will disappear forever, but some will remain throughout life and some will reemerge in old age. The reflexes that affect your baby most during swimming and bathing are described below. Most of them are outgrown by 6 months of age.

Swimming ''Amphibian'' Reflex

Even though your newborn's swimming reflex is primitive, it can propel the child for 1 or 2 feet. This reflex eventually loses strength and fades away, but if it is reinforced with practice in the tub and pool, it should be easier for your infant to make the transition from involuntary, reflexive swimming to voluntary, conscious swimming.

When your newborn is placed prone in the water, face submerged, the swimming reflex takes control of your baby's movement. Like an amphibian, your infant's arms and legs will rhythmically extend and flex while the torso will probably swing from side to side. This reflex is stimulated whenever your baby is placed face down on a flat surface, sometimes even on the bed. However, it is much stronger and more rhythmic when your infant is younger than 4 months, when the child is in a prone position unsupported in the water, and when the child is forced to hold its breath.

From 3 or 4 months of age to the time your baby learns to walk, the swimming reflex becomes disorganized and gradually disappears. During this phase, unless your infant has had lots of swimming practice, the child may sink below the surface without struggling or using any locomotive movement. If your baby has had swimming lessons, it's more likely your child will try to kick or pull to safety.

Righting Reflexes

When an infant is supine in the water, that is, lying in the back position, or when the child's head falls forward or backward, he or she will try to bring the head back to an upright position. The series of movements involved in this procedure are called righting reflexes. If you lay a baby who is between 4 months and 2-1/2 years old prone in the water, the child will try to remain in the stomach position with the head upright.

In babies who have learned to sit up, this attempt to keep upright can also be achieved by sitting up whenever they sense they are falling backward, as with the back float. But, if the child's head is supported when supine, the righting reflex usually is not stimulated and the baby will lie blissfully relaxed in the water.

When your infant is supine in the water, or when the child's head falls forward or backward, she will try to bring her head back to an upright position.

The righting reflex can play havoc with the back or supine position throughout childhood. Until about 2-1/2 years of age your baby's head should be supported whenever the child is supine. Your baby will feel more secure and less likely to feel as though he or she is falling. Drownproofing programs that require babies to stay on their backs unsupported ignore the compulsion of most infants to roll to the more upright stomach position.

Diving Response

While the swimming reflex causes your baby to move the arms, legs, and torso in a manner that propels the child through the water, the diving response causes your baby's lungs to stop inflating, heart to slow, and blood flow to be redistributed. The temporary cessation of breathing is called apnea, the slowing of the heart is called bradycardia, and the change in blood circulation is called redistribution of cardiac output.

The diving response is actually controlled by multiple reflexes rather than a single one. They each occur independently and to varying degrees, depending on the situation. Some babies have a strong diving response while others have none. The response tends to diminish with age. Animals other than humans also display the response. It can be stimulated in a variety of ways, but most commonly in babies it is stimulated whenever their faces are immersed in water.

The diving response causes changes in the distribution of circulating blood. In an above water situation, the normal blood flow brings nutrients and oxygen to all parts of the body and then collects waste products and carbon dioxide for disposal. When a person is unable to breathe, however, the blood does not receive new supplies of oxygen, nor can it get rid of carbon dioxide. As the supply of oxygen dwindles, the remaining oxygen must be conserved and utilized in the most efficient manner if life is to be sustained.

This conservation of oxygen is precisely what happens when the diving response is stimulated. The blood flow is changed to favor the most vital organs, by directing the remaining oxygen to the brain and the heart, away from the arms and legs. Fortunately, the tissues in the arms and legs can be deprived of oxygenated blood for 30 minutes or more without danger, whereas the brain and heart can only be deprived of blood for several minutes before suffering life threatening damage. The blood that remains in the body after breathing has stopped must be conserved in order to sustain the heart and brain for the longest time possible. Directing blood away from nonvital tissues to the brain and heart conserves oxygen so life can be prolonged.

As the amount of oxygen declines, metabolic processes that require oxygen must also slow down. Because their metabolism is depressed and their blood circulation conserves the remaining nutrients for the heart and brain, babies who are near drowning may appear dead but often can be revived. Thirty minutes is about the maximum time the organism can be deprived of oxygen, before true death occurs.

Babies do not have to be totally immersed to stimulate the diving response. Simple face immersion with breath-holding has the same effect of producing the diving response as does complete submersion. Breath-holding alone, though, elicits a much weaker response. Stimulation of the skin around the eyes and nose seems to be a very important component in eliciting the diving response. The skin does not even have to be wet, but the slowing of the heart is stronger if it is.

Cold water also strengthens the diving response, which is why some people submerged in cold water for long periods of time and presumed drowned are revived. Fear before immersion can also instigate the diving response and unconsciousness before immersion is thought to evoke a stronger diving response, possibly because the subconscious state of mind interferes less with reflexive processes.

Laryngospasm or Gag Reflex

If water accidently does get into your infant's mouth, it's unlikely to be aspirated or to cause choking. Instead, the gag reflex comes to the rescue, causing an involuntary spasm of the glottis and epiglottis, keeping water from entering the trachea, or windpipe. This watertight seal prevents inhalation of water into the lungs even when the water is already in the nose and mouth.

Like the diving reflex, which has been abused by those who use it to justify long and frequent submersions, the gag reflex has its limits. Even though it effectively closes off the windpipe for short periods of time, the gag reflex does not close off the esophagus, which leads to the stomach. Water may not end up in your baby's lungs, but it may find its way into the child's stomach and eventually cause water intoxication.

Moro Reflex

The Moro reflex is the cause of much of your baby's crying during the first 6 months of life, after which it disappears. When your baby hears a loud noise, is startled, or starts to fall, the Moro reflex takes over. Your infant will fling out its arms and legs, open its fingers, and then bring the arms inward, fingers curled, in an attempt to hug or catch onto something to stop the fall. At the same time, your baby cries to notify you that he or she is in trouble and needs rescuing.

If your baby is really falling, the Moro reflex is appropriate and fulfills a true need. More often, though, the reflex is stimulated when the child is not in real danger, such as when you lay your baby down for a nap. Undressing can also set off the Moro reflex. As you change your hand position, release your infant's head, or roll your baby sideways to remove clothing, your child's brain interprets the change in support as falling. The result is a Moro reflex and uncontrollable crying. Sudden changes of position or temperature can also evoke the response. One Moro reflex can even set off another, as the quick movements of the child's arms and legs during the first Moro restartle the baby and set off a second one.

Opportunities for the Moro reflex to be evoked during swimming or bathing are innumerable. Undressing, dressing, temperature changes, and the lack of solid support in the water can set off unending crying spells. Thank goodness, you need only to practice a few simple precautions to prevent the Moro reflex from making your baby's swimming and bathing experiences miserable!

Handle your baby carefully and securely. Hold the infant close to your body with as much of your baby's skin as possible touching yours. Restrain the child's arms (except when the child

During the Moro reflex, your baby will fling out her arms and legs.

is resting calmly in the back position, exhibiting the asymmetric tonic neck reflex) and encourage your baby to grasp your finger. Talk soothingly to your baby using a soft, moderately high-pitched voice. Whenever you change your infant's position, do so slowly. Never let your undressed newborn lie back without restraining at least one of the child's arms. If one of your baby's arms jerks away from the body, bring it slowly back in toward the chest. Keeping the child's head higher than the rest of the body also helps prevent the Moro reflex.

Swim or bathe only in warm water and immediately wrap the child in a towel after getting out. While in the water, hold your infant close to you most of the time. When moving the child to the back position, support the head securely with both hands or with your shoulder and extend your arms to support the rest of the child's body. When your child is in the prone position, support its chest with your palms and its chin with the heels of your palms. Make sure the water level always covers at least half of your baby's body. During submersion, do not jerk your infant out of the water. The maneuver should be slow and continuous and end with a secure hug.

The Moro reflex is the culprit in most crying during swimming and bathing, but its prevention is a delightful prescription: lots of love, hugs, and close body contact. What a marvelous way to learn how to swim!

⁻ *Shivering*

Most pools in the United States are kept too cool for babies. Water that is warm enough to keep your baby happy feels uncomfortably hot to lap swimmers. It's best to choose a pool where water temperature is kept between 88° and 94° to make sure your baby is happy and comfortable and runs no risk of hypothermia. Even in appropriately warm pools, your baby will experience some heat loss throughout the lesson. Usually your baby will remain warm and content for at least 30 minutes in the water, but if your child gets cold before that, it's time to leave.

Whenever your baby's brain senses that the body is chilled, it stimulates several reflexes. First, the blood vessels constrict, causing a reduced blood flow to the skin, which can withstand changes in temperature better than the body's interior. This surplus blood from the skin is then redirected in the body's interior to assure that the vital organs continue to function.

At this point, if your baby were an adult, he or she would start to shiver. The muscular activity that causes the shivering creates heat and helps to keep the body warm. Unlike an adult, though, your baby may not be able to shiver, so do not assume that the absence of shivering means your baby is warm. Newborns, especially, are rarely able to shiver. It has even been determined that 5% of all adults never shiver and may even feel comfortable, although their body temperature is rapidly falling.

How then can you tell when your baby is getting cold? There are several indicators besides shivering that indicate it's time to get out of the water. The child's lips may turn blue, as blood circulation to the skin is decreased. Your baby may pull the arms and legs up close to the body to reduce the amount of skin exposed to the cooling air and water. Or, your child may be very reluctant to move away from the warmth of your body.

Getting cold is no joke. It can lead to hypothermia. It's also unpleasant. A cold baby is simply not happy and alert. If you keep your baby in the water after the child gets cold, you only teach the child that swimming is uncomfortable. At the first sign your baby is chilled, get out and warm up.

Rooting Reflex

Nature provides your infant with the rooting reflex to ensure that milk is found. Whenever your baby's cheek or mouth is touched, the child will open its mouth and turn in the direction of the touch, seeking the mother's breast. If the source of nourishment is not found, your baby will cry in frustration. During dressing and water maneuvers, be careful not to accidently brush against your infant's cheek, unless you are prepared to offer the breast or bottle. Otherwise, you might be in for a long spell of crying.

Asymmetric Tonic Neck Reflex

Whenever your infant is lying quietly in the supine position, the child's head is usually to one side, with the arm on that side extended and the opposite leg bent at the knee. This poses no problem, unless you try to reposition your baby's body in the water so that the arms, legs, and head are all in alignment. Your baby will probably not be able to maintain a streamlined back float until at least 2-1/2 years of age.

Palmar Grasp Reflex

Whenever you place your finger on your baby's palm, your infant gives it a loving squeeze. This squeezing is due to the palmar grasp reflex. Not only is it a source of fun when playing with your baby, but it may help the child feel more secure when in the water. By placing your finger in your baby's hands during swimming or bathing, you provide the child with supplemental security and diminish the chances your baby will cry.

Flexor Withdrawal (Recoil) Reflex

The recoil reflex can sometimes be used to stimulate kicking in your infant. While supporting your baby in a prone or supine position, ask someone else to straighten one of the child's legs. This causes the leg to flex or recoil back toward the body and then extend again. By alternately straightening first one leg and then the other, the child may begin to kick. If you say "kick, kick, kick" during the recoil process, your baby will begin to associate the word kick with the physical sensation of kicking. Later when this reflex disappears, your baby may kick voluntarily whenever you say kick.

Your baby's arms are also controlled by this recoil reflex. Because of it, the child's arms are usually recoiled close to the body. Attempts to extend the arms are usually unsuccessful, as your baby stubbornly keeps the arms flexed. This flexion is so strong that you can almost lift the child into the air while the arms remain flexed. Because of this instinct to keep the arms next to the torso, your baby probably won't use the arms for pulling until at least a year old, when this reflex begins to fade.

Badkin's Reflex

If you firmly press your newborn's palms, your infant's mouth will automatically open. Obviously, you wouldn't want your child's mouth open underwater, so be careful you don't press your baby's palms during submersion. Although the gag reflex will prevent your baby from aspirating water, the child still can choke or swallow water.

4
Chapter

Your Baby's Physiological and Psychological Development

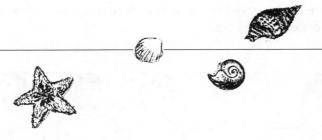

All babies are different. Each child reacts to swimming in a unique way, depending on disposition, age, body type, language ability, socialization, and current emotional state. In this chapter, learn how to adapt the lessons to the developmental characteristics of your own child.

Teach According to Your Baby's Maturational Level

Some swimming skills are more easily taught in the first 3 years of life, while others should not be taught until pubescence. Certain abilities are programmed by your baby's inborn, genetic timetable to emerge only at certain ages. Practicing such skills before the child's system is ready usually has a negligible effect. Sometimes it can even have a negative effect, such as when the child learns the skill in an artificial way. The resulting "splinter skill" interferes with proper learning later on.

Many abilities develop naturally in your baby; they do not have to be taught. What is difficult is determining what skills to teach and when. Whether you are teaching your baby by your-self or have the assistance of an instructor this chapter will help you make the right choices. From birth to 6 months a baby is primed to hold the breath and move the arms up and down in a primitive manner. Your baby is not programmed to use an ex-tended arm for pulling, the lower leg for kicking, or the head for lifting to get a breath.

At birth, your infant's head is one fourth of total body length, while an adult head comprises only one eighth of total length. The head circumference of your newborn is larger than the cir-cumference of the chest and it is not until age 1 year that chest circumference catches up.

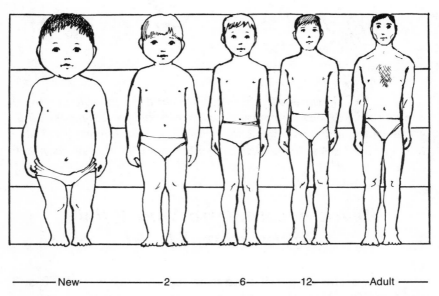

————— New————————2—————————6—————————12————————Adult ——————

At birth, your infant's head comprises one fourth of total body length, while an adult head comprises only one eighth of total length.

Because the child's head is so large and heavy compared to the rest of the body, it has a tendency to sink. This tendency is somewhat moderated by the fact that an infant's body is primarily made up of fat, which floats more readily than muscle and bone. The infant's arms and legs are relatively short, comprising only 25% of total length, whereas an adult's make up 50%. For this reason, kicking and pulling are fairly ineffectual for flotation and propulsion for infants.

As your baby matures and body proportions change, the child becomes ready to learn harder skills. The skills you should teach your child and the most appropriate ages at which they should be taught are described throughout the rest of this chapter.

1 to 4 Months

Physical characteristics: For the first several months, your infant's head is quite large in proportion to the rest of the child's body. This fact, together with the weakness of your baby's neck muscles, limits your child to holding the head up for only a few seconds at a time. Your infant's arm and leg movements are mostly random and rarely used for purposeful behavior. Most of the child's actions are involuntary and controlled by reflexes.

As your baby approaches 4 months of age, the child begins to acquire voluntary control of head, arm, and leg movements. When prone, the forearms are used as a head prop. When supine, the child's hands flutter enticingly overhead. Some babies find their feet just as fascinating as their hands and love to watch them sway overhead, from side to side.

As your infant's movements become more and more integrated, the child may surprise you by rolling over, first from the stomach to the back, later from the back to the stomach. While your infant's movements are being refined, so is the child's sense of touch. Too often this sense is thought of as being passive, one that doesn't change much from infancy to adulthood. Nothing could be further from the truth. If your baby is never touched or never gets a chance to experience a variety of sensations, the sense of touch can atrophy at a level far below its potential. Kittens and puppies, as well as human infants, need to have their sense of touch stimulated. They need to be licked, caressed, cuddled, and handled. The failure to thrive syndrome and even death have resulted from insufficient tactile stimulation. The bath and pool provide numerous opportunities to stimulate this sense, with the handling, hugging, and almost constant skin to skin contact.

Implications for swimming: Your infant needs lots of head support during the first 4 months, otherwise, the head will dip underwater. In the prone position, support the child's chin and chest securely with your palms. In the supine position, press the top of your baby's head against your chest or shoulder and support the rest of the child's body with your extended arms.

If the water is warm, your newborn will handle submersion as if he or she has been living in the water. By 4 months of age, though, your infant's natural affinity for the water will begin to fade. If you do not have access to a pool, practice in a tub filled with at least 6 inches of water.

If you do not have access to a pool, practice in a bathtub filled with at least 6 inches of water. (1 to 4 months)

Emotional characteristics: During the first 4 months of life your infant is totally dependent on you. The relationship is very one-sided, with you bestowing all the love, while your baby thanklessly seems to soak it up. Never use the word "selfish," though, to describe these thankless demands on your time. Consider them the bricks needed to build a healthy personality, one founded on trust.

Without trust, your child will have difficulty developing self-confidence, a concern for others, and lasting relationships. The more your infant can trust that you will always provide for his or her needs, the more secure the child will be in interactions with the surrounding environment. Your baby must have assurance that you will cushion falls and disappointments. If your infant is frequently frustrated because you are not around when needed, the child may worry and avoid facing new challenges.

Implications for swimming: Although it's impossible to know what babies think or feel, most psychologists warn against forcing your baby into traumatic situations, such as drownproofing classes.

Instead of building an association between water and fear, build one between water and enjoyment. If fond memories are created during your baby's first water experience, your infant will want to return for more swimming fun. You can create those memories by swimming in warm water, using lots of loving touches and praise, and keeping a bottle, breast, or pacifier handy during your baby's first bathing and swimming experiences.

Social characteristics: At birth, your baby is more attracted to human voices than other sounds. Before the first month of life is over, your infant seeks out your voice and eyes preferentially over those of other adults. Building a relationship with you is much more important to your child than intermittent encounters with others. Although at this age your baby willingly goes to other adults, the child wants to spend the majority of time with you.

Implications for swimming: At the pool, your infant should spend most of the lesson with you. However, this is also a good time to familiarize your baby with other adults. Babies less than 6 months old still accept being held by others. If you are part of a class, encourage your baby to get acquainted with the teacher. Hand your baby over to the teacher and step aside while they share a few private moments together. If you plan to continue lessons with the same teacher through at least 9 months of age, now is the best time for your infant to begin adjusting to that teacher. Just remember to keep those encounters brief.

Intellectual characteristics: As early as 2 months of age, your infant begins to associate certain actions, sights, and sounds with particular needs and responses. While watching you prepare a bottle or prepare to breastfeed, your child may anticipate eating by making eager mouth movements or excited gestures.

Associations like these form your baby's first learning experiences. Within a few weeks, the child will accumulate a large collection of these associations. Those that have a strong impact or are repeated will be remembered.

Implications for swimming: After your baby's first submersions, the child begins to associate going underwater with movement toward the water's surface. It only takes two or three such experiences for your baby to learn to hold its breath whenever pushed toward the water. But just as easily as this association is learned, it can be forgotten if all types of submersion are discontinued for 2 or 3 months. This does not mean you should enroll your infant in continuous pool lessons. It only means that your baby's learned breath holding must be reinforced with regular submersions, either in the bath or the pool, if the breath holding is to remain a part of your child's performance repertoire.

Parent's role: Many doctors are reluctant to recommend formal swimming lessons for infants between birth and 4 months of age. This reluctance stems from the inherent vulnerability of infants in the first 4 months of life. For most infants, early swim lessons pose no health problems. For those with developmental problems, the hazards are unknown. Because it's not always obvious yet which infants may have problems, physicians often are reluctant to recommend formal swimming lessons. Your pediatrician may want to observe your infant carefully during those fragile first 4 months before allowing pool lessons.

Actually, what your child is primed to learn about swimming at this age can be provided almost as easily in a bathtub as in a pool. The main value of swimming lessons at this age is to keep your baby exposed to the water before the child's inborn swimming reflexes disappear. For the first several months of life, the bathtub provides an adequate place to meet this goal. Your baby will probably accept formal swimming lessons more readily if the child is not given the chance to forget the prebirth sensations of water surrounding the body. Gentle, early water experience also helps to build a positive attitude. The emphasis here is on the word "gentle." Swimming experiences for babies this age should resemble a soothing, sensual massage more than purposeful skill instruction.

5 to 8 Months

Physical characteristics: Usually by 6 months of age, your baby can control head movements without your help, but the head is still quite large in comparison with the rest of the child's body. Many of the child's newborn reflexes have disappeared and been replaced by purposeful actions. No longer do your baby's arms and legs seem to have a mind of their own. Instead, your child consciously uses the arms and legs to reach for specific toys. By 8 months, your baby can move toys from hand to hand.

When lying supine, infants may lift their heads to look at their feet. Enough control has been developed at 5 to 8 months for children to grab their feet and stuff them into their mouths. Babies can kick vigorously enough to move, usually backward, across the floor or bed. Rolling over is also becoming voluntary, and babies will roll from front to back or vice versa whenever they want a change of scenery.

Implications for swimming: Head, arm, and leg proportions are such that the child is still top heavy, making independent floating and swimming for propulsion a real struggle. The child may be able to maintain an independent back float, but it is an unnatural position at this age. When practicing the back position, be sure to support your baby's head. If allowed to lie unsupported in the water, most babies this age will try to roll over to a prone position. The unsupported supine position is contrary to their natural tendencies.

In the prone position, your infant's neck muscles are strong enough that chin support is no longer needed. If you place a toy out of reach, your baby may try to get it by stretching, kicking, or scooting forward. Extended arm movements, however, remain limited, and most children still find it unnatural to fully

When practicing the back position, be sure to support your baby's head. (5 to 8 months)

extend their arms in the water to make pulling movements. Leg movement varies. Kicking may be nonexistent or vigorous. Even when vigorous, though, it's not efficient for long swims.

Emotional characteristics: Too young to get around, yet always wanting to be where the action is, your baby clamors to be carried everywhere you go. The child enjoys being handled and wants to be in the middle of everything you do.

By 8 months, your child's attachment to the main caregiver peaks in a stage referred to as separation anxiety. This stage starts developing as early as 6 months, but on the average is strongest at 8 months. While separation anxiety usually subsides before age 10 months, it may recur around 13 to 14 months.

Implications for swimming: Although separation anxiety is a fact of life in most children's development, it does not have to interfere with swimming lessons. As long as your baby is with you and the teacher or other adults remain in the background, the child is usually eager to go anywhere and do anything you request, including submerging. Starting formal swimming lessons at this age usually works out well.

Social characteristics: Socialization blossoms between 5 and 8 months of age. When you or others smile, look at, and listen to your baby, the child will return the attention by babbling, smiling, and watching your every move. By 6 months of age, your baby has learned that it's more fun to be played with than to be left alone, even in a room brimful of toys. Other persons are fascinating, but given a choice, your baby still prefers parental companionship to that of the teacher or other playmates.

Implications for swimming: If you are part of a class or swimming with others, introduce your baby to the other children and adults. As your child becomes accustomed to them he or she will look forward to greeting them and will accept them as a normal part of the classroom scene. While it's not a requirement to hand your baby over to the teacher or other parents, encourage some communication and some physical contact with them. With perseverance, your baby eventually will learn to trust others.

Intellectual characteristics: Your baby's appetite is voracious when it comes to learning. It's hard to provide your infant with the constant flow of stimulation the child constantly demands. Attention span is still short, averaging only 5 to 7 seconds per interaction, so your baby seems to be continually searching for new items to examine. When a new item is found, it goes straight to the mouth for further investigation. Quickly bored when left too long in one position, your baby will demand frequent changes in perspective. Fortunately, many of these changes your child will be able to handle without help, having mastered rolling over, sitting up, or scooting.

Implications for swimming: Boredom during lessons is often the cause of crying at this age. To keep up with your baby's need to explore, be adventuresome. Change your baby's swimming positions often and wander around the pool searching for new toys and experiences.

Parent's role: Until your baby has overcome separation anxiety, expect to be responsible for most of the actual teaching in a baby swim class. All of the eight basic skills (see chapter 6) can be practiced at this age, but don't expect your baby to master them.

Bring favorite floating toys to the pool for chewing on or swimming to. Encourage vocalization by carrying on meaningful conversations with your baby. Even though your baby's babbling is unintelligible, show interest in the child's attempts to communicate.

9 to 12 Months

Physical characteristics: Clutching the sofa determinedly, your baby pulls up to stand, then breaks into a broad grin as if to say, ''I did it myself! I don't need Mom or Dad to get around.'' Between 9 and 12 months, babies learn how to get just about anywhere they want to go. Children's arms are strong enough to pull themselves up to stand. The legs can support their entire weight for long periods of time. They are coordinated enough to move all four limbs reciprocally. Most babies this age can crawl and some have already learned how to walk.

Your baby no longer is content to passively lie back and wait for your return. The child prefers being upright to see where you are. If you move to another room, your baby will either follow along behind, or clamor to be carried.

Most of the time babies keep their arms close to their chests. Although they can reach for a toy, after retrieval they will bring the toy back in close to the body. This holding of the arms close to the body is, to some extent, reflexive, and it's hard to pull the child's arms away from the body. Nursemaid's elbow, a common malady at this age, develops when a baby is pulled with one arm to stand. Although the child's physician can correct the problem with a simple maneuver, the condition can be avoided by lifting under both arms, thereby distributing the child's weight evenly.

By 12 months of age, your baby probably will have passed through the disorganized swimming phase and will again make swimming movements when placed prone in the water. Unlike the reflexive swimming movements your infant made shortly after birth, these movements are voluntary.

The child's arms are strong enough to pull herself up to stand. (9 to 12 months)

Implications for swimming: It's frustrating for your baby to try to interact with the world when lying flat on his or her back. Therefore, do not expect your baby to like the back position. However, the child does need to learn how to back float for safety reasons, so persist in your efforts even though most back practice will be short-lived. Just be sure to support your baby's head whenever the child is in the back position.

At this age, practice in the stomach position complements your baby's development more than the back position. The reciprocal arm and leg movements your baby is using for crawling follow the same pattern used for swimming. Now is a prime time to practice swimming between you and the teacher or another adult.

Emotional characteristics: By this time your baby has become skilled in reading your thoughts and feelings. Those thoughts and feelings should be mostly positive and convince your child you are pleased with his or her accomplishments. This is the age when your child begins to use accomplishments to build self-confidence. Many of your baby's experiences will end in failure and be a drain on your baby's self-confidence, so the child continually needs to be reminded that he or she is doing a fine job.

The foundation for your baby's self-confidence begins in infancy, but between 8 and 12 months of age, your child probably will experience a surge in self-confidence. This is mainly a result of your baby's efforts to get around alone and to master the environment without your help. Your baby will also be leaving behind the separation anxiety stage and will be establishing a separate identity. Together, these factors culminate in a growth spurt of self-confidence.

While your baby is beginning to separate from you and explore new areas, the child will still get pleasure from familiar facets of the environment. Your baby is now old enough to have become accustomed to many of the sights and sounds he or she is exposed to daily. Because your baby can predict the outcome of many of these daily events, your child feels in control and, consequently, self-confident. At this age, it's as important to provide your baby with familiar, predictable events as it is to provide new and different experiences.

Implications for swimming: Help your baby build self-confidence by showing approval of accomplishments with smiles, hugs, and encouraging words. If your child is accustomed to swimming lessons, self-confidence will come from repeating previously mastered skills, as well as from attempting more challenging ones. If your baby has not been swimming before, self-confidence in the water will come more slowly. In the first several lessons, provide your baby with easy tasks, ones you are sure the child can master. That way, your child has a new set of successes after each lesson to help develop self-confidence in the water.

While the time between 9 and 12 months of age is ripe for building self-confidence, it is also ripe for cultivating fears. One of the easiest ways of instilling fear of the water is to push your baby into water experiences the child is not yet ready to handle. For the first several lessons limit practice to above-water skills practice. You may wish to try minidunks, but only if you're fairly confident your baby won't be frightened.

Another problem that develops at this age with a newcomer to swimming lessons centers around how the child sees the roles of the mother and father. By now your baby has become accustomed to the roles Mom and Dad play. In one parent's arms, the child may react by clinging, expecting to be shielded from this strange, new experience called swimming. In the other parent's arms, the swimming experience may be greeted as an exciting adventure. For this reason, some children react more positively to the water if the least protective parent takes them to swimming lessons.

Social characteristics: Although your baby may still hide against your shoulder when a stranger approaches, the child's curiosity is beginning to overpower shyness. From the safety of your arms your child may eagerly perform for any admiring audience. Your baby may also imitate the antics of both strangers and close acquaintances.

Implications for swimming: Take advantage of your baby's desire to perform for and imitate others. When another child demonstrates a skill, watch with your baby and clap or "patty cake" together to applaud the other child's efforts. When it's your baby's turn to perform, hopefully the other parents and babies will return the compliment by cheering on and applauding your child, too. Babies at this age love clapping games. Peek-a-boo and waving bye-bye are other popular pastimes. Playing them with the teacher or other children in class will help your baby to build friendships.

Like many forces in your child's life, imitation has both a good and bad side. On the good side, it enables your baby to learn new skills simply by watching another child do them first. On the bad side, your baby may start to cry and develop a fear of the water when observing a fearful child's avoidance reaction. If another child starts crying, move away and distract your baby with a game or skill practice. Seek out happy babies for your child to be near and to imitate.

Intellectual characteristics: Language is now becoming meaningful to your youngster. The child understands many more words than he or she can say. By 9 months, your child knows the meaning of "no," "mom," "dad," and what his or her name is. By 12 months, your baby can carry out simple commands like, "Get your teddy bear."

Despite this surge in language development, your baby's most obvious achievement at this age is in the area of eye-hand coordination. When your child is interested in something, your baby can reach for it, turn it over to get a better look, or move it to a different place. Your child has also mastered the complex, reciprocal movement of the arms and legs for crawling.

Implications for swimming: Your baby will learn the meaning of words you repeat during swimming lessons. Consistently say "kick, kick, kick," whenever you move your baby's legs up and down. Use the word "pull" when you move your child's arms in a pulling motion. Say "swim to Mommy" or Daddy when the teacher pushes your baby underwater to you. By 12 months, your baby may learn to kick, pull, and swim whenever commanded to do so.

Although the motion used to crawl on land is slightly different from that used in the water, the movements are similar enough to be complementary. The reciprocal nature of the arm and leg movement is the same on both land and water. Because the water helps support your child's body when swimming, muscle development of the arms and legs sometimes proceeds more rapidly. That is why swimming is so often a part of the physical therapy used in rehabilitating handicapped children.

Parent's role: On the way to the pool tell your baby you are going to swimming lessons. Describe what skills you will practice and who you will see. Include references to time like, "First we will undress and then we will get in the water." Talk about the people you will see and refer to the other parents and babies by using their first names. Hearing their names primes your baby for seeking out the familiar faces of friends again. Such talk also increases your baby's vocabulary and prepares the child for what is going to happen, helping him or her feel more in control of the situation and less anxious.

If your baby is just starting lessons, fortify yourself with lots of patience. At this age your baby prefers the familiar and may be cautious and fearful in new situations. If you don't push your child into skill mastery and instead play familiar, nonthreatening games, such as Patty Cake, your baby will accept the pooltime as a welcome activity.

Use the word "yes" more than "no" during the lesson. To your baby, the word "no" signifies that you have control. For some children that serves as a catalyst for rebellion. Children who hear only "no" have trouble learning that "yes" or a positive response is a legitimate way to answer, too. So say "yes" as much as possible and allow your child some independence in choosing swimming activities.

13 to 16 Months

Physical characteristics: "Energy unlimited" aptly describes your baby now. The child has mastered walking, crawling, and climbing. If you would permit it, your child would explore every square inch of your home. Climbing is a favorite activity, and there seems to be no limit to the heights your baby can attain. Children continually test the physical limitations of their muscles and abilities. At this age, children's gross motor skills zoom ahead, leaving fine motor skills plodding along behind in the dust.

Implications for swimming: Trying to limit your baby's physical activity only frustrates the child. The drive to perfect gross motor skills is quite strong. On the other hand, if you allow your baby unlimited territory in which to frolic, you invite falls, tears, and frustration from failures. The happy medium between overrestriction and unlimited freedom lies in confining your baby to a large, safety-proofed part of the pool.

Emotional characteristics: Although your baby is busy challenging the physical limits of the environment, emotionally the child prefers to stay close to you. The child has not yet had enough worldly experience to have discovered lots of conflicting alternatives to your plans. If you do not confuse your baby with lots of choices, your child will be content with the choice you offer. In making choices, your baby's primary desire is to please you. This is what makes your toddler feel important and needed. Most often your baby will go along with whatever you want to do. If your child does have a different opinion, it is usually easy to accommodate your baby's simple requests.

While it is best not to offer too many alternatives, do give your baby some choice in choosing activities. The self-confidence children gain from making decisions on their own is a valuable emotional attribute. As your baby's self-confidence begins to flourish, your child becomes aware of being a separate person from you. Your baby realizes that he or she has at least some power to control what happens. At this age forays into the world of independence are brief, as your toddler fluctuates between wanting to be independent and being dependent on you to satisfy most needs.

Implications for swimming: It is important to give toddlers ample opportunities to build self-confidence in their swimming abilities. Let them decide whether to swim to the wall, to another adult, or to you. Structure the choices so that whichever one your baby chooses is not only acceptable to you, but also will not frustrate the child. If toddlers are provided with more than one choice, they won't feel compelled to devise their own, probably less desirable alternatives to display independence. By treating your baby as an important person whose choices you respect, you build a self-confident, positively motivated toddler.

Social characteristics: Your 13- to 16-month-old can be beguiling with others. Your child is lovable, friendly, and sociable. Although some toddlers go through another stranger anxiety phase around this time, the anxiousness is usually short-lived and soon overcome by the desire for attention from others. Most often strangers are viewed as being intriguing rather than enemies. As long as you are there to provide a secure emotional base, your toddler happily makes brief forays into the outside world.

Games with one other person are favorite activities now. Your baby loves to be chased and caught. Your baby likes being the center of attention, and if you show you enjoy your child's "performance," your toddler will repeat the show over and over.

Implications for swimming: As long as you are nearby, your youngster most likely will enjoy going with the teacher or another adult for a minute or two. However, your child probably would be anxious if left totally alone with another person. Your baby will be more content in a swimming class in which you handle most of the instruction.

Play games like Peek-a-boo and Humpty Dumpty. Let your toddler hang onto the side of the pool while you pretend to sneak up and surprise him or her. Laugh with and praise the performance of your baby.

Intellectual characteristics: By the time your baby is 16 months old, the child understands much more than he or she can communicate. Sometimes your toddler may cry from the frustration of knowing what he or she wants, yet not being able to verbalize it. Your baby has lots of thoughts to share with you but is not adept enough with language to always make you understand. Your child probably does understand what the eyes, nose, ears, and mouth are, and can imitate you by pointing out these common body parts.

When imitating skills, your baby usually can imitate only a short part of the procedure rather than a long sequence, but simple games that teach parts of the body and searching for hidden toys are well within your baby's abilities. Toys have become more than objects just to chew, look at, or hold. Your toddler prefers playthings that can be manipulated by emptying or filling or squeezing to make noise.

Implications for swimming: Even though your baby has difficulty communicating with you, give full attention to the attempts. It is frustrating enough for your child not to be able to fully express what he or she wants, but if you don't listen, your child may decide that learning to talk is just not worth the effort. By trying to understand what your toddler is saying, the child will see talking as a worthwhile skill to practice.

Now is a good time to take advantage of your youngster's natural tendency to learn by imitation. Point to your own nose then ask your child to find his or her own. Move your arms in a pulling motion and encourage your baby to imitate. Demonstrate the skills your child should practice by either doing them yourself or watching another child. If the skill is complicated, chances are your baby will only copy part of it, so keep your demonstration simple.

Provide toys that make noise or can be emptied or filled, like plastic cups, bowls, and strainers. Your baby can spend hours just filling and pouring. Wind-up toys that swim through the water are also good choices, even though your baby will want to retrieve them for closer observation before the toy has had a chance to "swim" very far.

Parent's role: "I'm available if you need me" is a good motto to follow when your baby is between 13 and 16 months. At this age, inconsistency is a normal aspect of your toddler's need for you. One moment your child may want to be held close and the next moment to run around free of your presence. It's hard to tell whether your baby's up-to-the-minute need is for dependence or independence, so listen closely to your baby's words and body language to determine your role.

This is also an age where you need to curb your use of the word "no." "No" has a powerful effect on your toddler's daily life, so it's not surprising your child finds it intriguing. Label-

"I'm available if you need me" is a good motto to follow when your baby is between 13 to 16 months.

ing a situation as a "no, no" may have the opposite reaction you want by making it more fascinating for your child. Instead of saying "no" all the time, set limits by providing your baby with other choices or by removing either the "no, no" or your child.

17 to 20 Months

Physical characteristics: Although your toddler has mastered many gross motor sequences, such as walking or crawling, mastery of fine motor movements lags behind. The child's legs and arms still function basically as single units, with little ability to differentiate movements of the fingers, hands, toes, and feet. Similarly, your youngster may move the entire head instead of just the eyes to see an object slightly to the right or left. When walking, the whole body may tilt forward together with the leading leg.

Implications for swimming: While your child can kick and pull, the fine motor movements of the feet, knees, hips, and hands are still too undifferentiated and stiff for significant propulsion. For this reason, a simultaneous arm pull, similar to the breast stroke, sometimes works better. Because your baby has difficulty differentiating knee movements from those of the entire leg, the child will also need your help in jumping into the water from the side.

Usually this lack of differentiation is a hindrance, but in the case of the back float, it is a plus. Since your baby often moves the entire head instead of the eyes only, simply by asking your child to look at you when lying supine, your toddler may roll the entire head back along with the eyes and thereby align the body in the proper back float position. While in the back position, toddlers may lie with their arms touching their shoulders. This helps some children feel more secure and helps to maintain a steadier body balance while back floating. Most children this age still need the security of their parent's hands supporting them while back floating.

Emotional characteristics: Up to now you have probably heard other parents describe their children's temper tantrums, but you may never have seen one in your own child. Now is the time to prepare yourself. Around 1-1/2 years of age, your toddler may respond to a frustrating situation by having a tantrum. Fortunately, these first tantrums are usually short-lived if you try to distract the youngster before the tantrum becomes full blown.

At this age, your baby is fascinated by its surroundings, and throughout the day the child will continually switch from one activity to another. In the midst of this constant stream of changes, your child still needs a sense of stability and may drag a familiar object, such as a security blanket, along wherever he or she goes. Your baby also needs you to be a stabilizing force, so concentrate on reacting consistently.

Occasionally, your toddler may get into a predicament and become frightened. For this reason, you may notice your baby acquiring new fears, such as fear of the bathtub. Fear of the bathtub is usually unrelated to swimming. If you react with calmness and assure the child that the situation is under control, the fear will usually be overcome. Do not ignore the child's fears, though, and force your baby back into the situation too soon, or the fear may become more embedded.

At this age, your baby is fascinated by her surroundings and throughout the day will continually switch from one activity to another. (17 to 20 months)

Implications for swimming: Structure your toddler's swimming environment so that the child encounters only those challenges and experiences you know can be managed. You must also protect your baby from impulsively forging ahead into frustrating situations.

Of course, despite your precautions, your baby may still encounter a frightening swimming experience. Because the experience is still in its initial stages of fear formation, it need not haunt your baby throughout life. First, assure your child that the frightening situation is past and all is well. Second, distract your toddler with an activity you know he or she enjoys and can handle. Third, avoid the situation until your baby has rebuilt self-confidence and is ready to try again.

If your toddler feels better carrying a security blanket or toy let your child bring it to the pool, but firmly explain that it must be left in the locker room or at the side of the pool when the lesson starts. Let your child choose the place to store the toy so that your baby feels some control over it.

Social characteristics: Your baby's new sense of independence from you also can be observed in the area of social development. You are no longer your child's only reason for living. Your toddler is also fascinated by other adults and children.

While learning to control the surrounding environment and the inanimate objects in it, your baby also learns how to be assertive in interactions with live opponents. Your baby is not about to forfeit any power to peers. Sharing toys is unusual. More than likely your baby will gather all the pool toys into a private pile. It does not matter if your child wants to play with them or not. Your baby's concern is with controlling the world, and the child does not want to share that power with anyone else. Your baby may find other children fascinating to watch, mainly because your child covets their toys.

Implications for swimming: Classtime usually proceeds more smoothly if no toys are around for the children to fight over. Because toddlers are far enough into teething that they really don't need a toy to chew on during the lesson, nor do they have to have a favorite toy with them constantly, postponing toy play until the end of the lesson is usually an acceptable procedure. If there is toy play during free time, make sure your toddler has one in each hand. With both hands full, the child is less likely to grab another baby's toy.

Intellectual characteristics: Verbal communication and noises hold a tremendous fascination for your toddler. The child wants you to label and name familiar objects. If you ask your baby to fetch a certain object, the child feels very important when fulfilling your request. Animal noises are also interesting, and your baby may be able to mimic their sounds, though at the same time unable to say their names. Keep in mind, though, that your baby's attention span is still short. While the child enjoys making sounds and hearing new words, after a few minutes of concentrated practice, your toddler will be ready to move on to something else.

Implications for swimming: During swimming lessons when you want to distract your toddler from a forbidden activity or whenever you want the child's attention, make a noise, such as the mooing of a cow or the barking of a dog. Once you have your baby's attention use verbal directions together with a physical demonstration of what you want your baby to do. If you keep the directions simple, your toddler most likely will understand and try to please you by complying with your request.

Parent's role: By now your baby has learned to get your attention not only by pleasing you, but also by disagreeing. In fact, disagreeing may be even more fun because your baby sees it as a way of controlling you, just as you control your baby. Allow your child some power in choosing what to do during swimming lessons, in order to help satisfy the need to control.

Hopefully, the need for power can be satisfied by allowing your child the chance to tell you what to do during free time. During this time, be as inconspicuous as possible and let your child choose the activities and give the orders. If those activities lead to conflict with another baby, step in to help only after the children have had a chance to solve the problem on their own.

21 to 24 Months

Physical characteristics: Continual movement continues to be your baby's primary physical focus. This constant exercise plays a big role in your child's increasing muscular strength and endurance. Games where your toddler can use this strength, such as those involving jumping and acceleration, are becoming favorites.

Most toddlers this age also are becoming aware of their genitals. For most of their short lives, their genitals were out of sight under a diaper, or out of reach of their short arms. As their arms lengthen and as diapers give way to training pants, these unexplored areas become a prime target for their curiosity.

Implications for swimming: Provide opportunities for your baby to utilize emerging strength and endurance. The child may enjoy jumping off a low diving board into your arms or going down a slide. If the slide is high, set your baby near the bottom, before sliding the child off the end. The teacher or another adult should be waiting to catch the child to cushion the force of the jump as soon as your toddler hits the water.

In the back position let your baby feel strength in the legs by placing the child's feet against the side and counting to 3 as the child pushes against the wall to propel his or her body further into the water. Kicking, whether front or back, is also becoming a source of delight for your toddler. Your child may find it thrilling to kick forcefully through the water leaving a trail of geyser-like splashes.

After the lesson is over and your toddler is waiting to be dressed, the child may fill up the time with harmless genital exploration. This is quite normal, and unless it becomes your child's dominant form of entertainment, should not be a reason to worry.

Emotional characteristics: Your baby's need to control and dominate continues as the child nears age 2. Children become very possessive with their toys and bodies and may become angry whenever their "turf" is invaded. Simply touching your child or putting his or her clothes in the washing machine invites an emotional outburst. Your toddler may also perceive direct commands as a challenge, so unless you want to argue, make your requests indirect. For example, say, "The toy chest is empty; let's fill it," rather than "Pick up your toys."

Implications for swimming: It may seem that you and your toddler cannot agree on anything. All of your requests during swimming lessons are met by your baby's firm refusal. As discouraging as this stage appears, it has its bright side. The situation can be compared to finding a pair of pants that fit. You may have to try on quite a few pairs before finding the size, color, and style that flatter you most. Similarly, before your baby can find the best place on the continuum between dependence and independence, the child must discover by trial and error the limits in which he or she is most comfortable. Be patient and your baby will learn, without any help from you, that always saying no to you does not serve his or her interests best.

Until your toddler learns this, handle your requests indirectly. Say, ''Let's swim to the side,'' instead of ''Swim to the side for me.'' If the response is a refusal to swim to the wall because your baby wants to play Humpty Dumpty, compromise and say ''OK, you may do another Humpty Dumpty, and then swim to the wall.'' A response like this protects your toddler's ego and allows the child some power. It also maintains your position as the parent with the right to make the final decision.

Social characteristics: Between 21 and 24 months of age, your baby's social skills may seem to regress. No longer does the child

Most of your child's play is solitary. (21 to 24 months)

want to please others. No longer do you wonder if your child is overly attached to you. The child seems too independent and power-hungry to become attached to anyone! Those quiet moments of cuddling you used to share are becoming fewer and fewer.

But just as you are ready to conclude that your baby is antisocial, watch for an indication that the child's self-centeredness is fading. Even though your toddler still doesn't like to share, your child does have an idea of what belongs to you and to other children and, surprisingly, may passively acquiesce when another child's toy is returned to its owner. If your baby has two toys, one may even be given to another child who has none. Now that the child has mastered the meaning of "mine," he or she is starting to learn the meaning of "yours."

Implications for swimming: As long as socializing with others does not interfere with your toddler's own plans, the child will probably submit to playing some group swimming games. If your child knows the game, the children, and other parents, the activity may even be part of your toddler's plan for the lesson.

Most of your child's play is solitary, though. During free time, your child will spend most of the time playing alone and watching the other children. Your toddler may copy what another is doing but rarely will go over to that child and play cooperatively.

Intellectual characteristics: As babies near 2 years of age, they become enamored with the properties of water. Even if your child is not in swimming lessons, water still has a special attraction. Your toddler enjoys having you around to watch these water experiments and observe what is being learned.

At this age, your toddler may be talking. While most babies know some words, some are speaking in short sentences. Whatever your child's speaking level, it is important to listen and talk to your baby about what is being learned. Not only does your toddler learn by watching others or actually doing an activity, your child also learns by talking and thinking about it.

Implications for swimming: Swimming is not all your baby learns at the pool. The child also learns about the properties of water.

Make sure the toy basket has lots of items that your toddler can use to experiment with the water. Sponges, bubble pipes, strainers, funnels, and turkey basters are just a sample of the many items from which you can choose.

Talk with your baby about what is happening during these water experiments. The child may not know all the words you use, but by associating them with what is observed, your child will eventually figure out their meaning.

Parent's role: Many, but not all, of your baby's interactions with others are negative. In between those negative moments, the child can be cooperative, especially when your baby feels important and competent. Letting your toddler help with household chores is an excellent way of enhancing the child's sense of importance and competence. Provide lots of opportunities for your baby to show how much he or she knows.

On swimming day, let your child pack the swimming bag and dress and undress without your help. During the lesson, do not tell your child everything to do. Instead, ask if your child can help do a task. As long as you see your role as an admirer of your baby's competence, the child will most likely do precisely what you want.

25 to 28 Months

Physical characteristics: As your child's body matures and takes on a more efficient shape for physical activity, your baby will discover new ways to move—ways you did not know were possible. The child may crawl through culverts, climb onto a shelf in a closet, or into a drawer. To a toddler, exploring the relationship between his or her body and the space around it is very exciting.

Implications for swimming: Your child's arms and legs may be long enough now to support the body in an independent back float. Not all babies this age are capable of doing this, depending on their body proportions, swimming experience, and confidence. If you want to try it with your toddler, be sure to keep your hands close to the child's head so you can give support whenever it is needed.

Your baby may also be able to hold its breath long enough to dive to the bottom of the pool, retrieve an object, and regain footing, all without your assistance. Underwater games such as this may become your child's favorite swimming activities, as they provide new ways to explore the water environment. Swimming through your legs or diving into a hoop are especially fun for accomplished 2-year-olds.

If you want to try an independent back float with your toddler, be sure to keep your hands close to the child's head so you can give support whenever it is needed. (25 to 28 months)

Emotional characteristics: Although your youngster still wants to be held when frightened or injured, the child prefers to spend most of the day independent of your control. Negative behavior, in the form of saying no and refusing to comply with your wishes, is at its peak now. It's getting harder to distract your toddler from forbidden activities.

Being permissive and giving in to your child only lengthen this negative period. Your toddler will be happier and will pass through this stage quicker in an environment where the limits and rules are well known. If you do not provide limits, your baby will continue to test you until you do. It's much easier if you set appropriate limits before trouble occurs.

Implications for swimming: Try to foresee situations your child may want to challenge and modify them before trouble develops. For example, your baby might have a toy that no one else may touch. If your child refuses to part with it, instead of bringing it to class and risking a fight with another child over it or a tantrum when you have to take it away during swimming time, explain that it must be left at home. If the child is adamant about taking it along, it may be necessary to hide the object long enough before leaving home so your youngster forgets about it.

Know the rules and limits of the class, so that the first time your toddler strays too far you know when to react. If running is not allowed, be prepared to immediately stop your child whenever he or she starts to break into a run. Insist on obedience when you judge it to be important, especially for safety's sake. On the other hand, if your child's behavior is not dangerous, it may be wiser to permit the child to continue. If you are too strict, your toddler may never learn the valuable lesson that sometimes it's all right to change your mind.

Social characteristics: While sharing with other babies is still rare, your toddler may share toys or snacks with a doll or stuffed toy during pretend play. To a 2-year-old, socializing with dolls is often more fun than playing with peers. Perhaps because the dolls do not talk back or say no, your child finds they make better playmates than unpredictable real-life kids.

Implications for swimming: Playing with other children may not be on your child's list of things to do at swimming lessons; however, playing games alongside of them probably is. Your toddler may like repeating familiar games and may patiently wait for a turn. Because swimming class provides your toddler with many such games, it encourages your child to reach out and interact with peers.

If your toddler has a waterproof doll, consider bringing it to class. Whatever the doll does, your child may want to try, too. The child may readily perform skills that are normally avoided if the doll does them first. For example, if your child refuses to join hands with the other children in "Ring Around the Rosies," have the doll join hands with the other children first and then with your child.

Intellectual characteristics: Your toddler may now be talking, but the child still needs to be shown, as well as told, how to do things. The best way to teach your child is with an activity that combines both motor and verbal elements, such as acting out nursery rhymes. Children this age love simple songs and once your toddler learns one, it will be sung over and over.

Implications for swimming: Nursery rhymes are a great way to teach new swimming skills and to reinforce old ones. For example, your baby has probably been underwater many times now. While the child may not be frightened when underwater, he or she may be bored. To make underwater practice more fun, sing "Ring Around the Rosies" and go underwater after the words "all fall down." You can create your own rhymes, too, to teach your toddler new skills. They may not become hit records, but they can be effective in teaching your baby how to swim.

Parent's role: Your focal point during swimming lessons should be your toddler. Adopt the attitude that the pool is a fun place to learn. Your toddler will be less likely to have a temper tantrum while busy having fun and being lavished with praise. If your youngster gets the idea that the lessons are just another way for you to show your control, you will not get cooperation.

29 to 32 Months

Physical characteristics: Finally, your child's fine motor coordination has improved enough to be noticeable. Your toddler can walk on tiptoes, jump with both feet, and stand on one foot. The child has enough control over hand and finger movements to move them separately without involving the whole arm.

Implications for swimming: The wide range of movements that your toddler has mastered on land can be practiced in the water, too. A fun way of doing this is for the child to pretend to be different animals. While in the shallow end, tell your child to hop like a rabbit across the pool, thereby practicing jumping with both feet. Pretend to be a cat and walk around the pool on tip-toe, meowing while your child follows you pretending to be your kitten. Gallop and whinny like a horse, swim like a fish, or stalk around the pool like a hungry shark. The movements your child uses in pretending to be these different animals will be more varied and allow more opportunities for coordination improvement than practicing only the eight basic skills.

Emotional characteristics: The payoff of early swimming lessons is becoming obvious, especially in the area of emotional growth. Compared to children who have not had any type of physical exercise class, your child may seem more eager to meet new challenges, more willing to wait for a turn, and more confident in teacher-pupil relationships.

By now, much of your toddler's negativism is being replaced by a desire to cooperate. At home, your offspring may love to help you with household chores, such as mopping the floor, making the bed, and watering the plants. Your youngster wants to be like you. Although with your child's help simple household tasks can turn into major messes, the more you let the child help, the more likely your toddler will grow up to be a helpful member of the family. The more you let your toddler have some control over your work by helping, the more likely your baby will let you have some guiding control in his or her world.

Implications for swimming: If your baby has been having fun in swimming, playing alongside the other children, chances are your child is now beginning to seek out their approval. Although most of your toddler's conversation is directed toward adults, your child does enjoy watching what the other children are doing and likes them to watch back. To get their attention, your toddler may act silly or splash around the pool.

Along with these increasing attempts to socialize come inevitable personality clashes with other children. At this age the best solution is just to keep the two children apart. A lengthy lecture simply will not be understood. Logical explanations are practically worthless.

Social characteristics: Children between 29 and 32 months exhibit social characteristics similar to those of children between 25 and 28 months. See page 68 for a more detailed description.

Intellectual characteristics: Your toddler's preference for using the left or right hand is now becoming apparent. Although the child is not consistent in that preference, the hand that is predominantly used in coloring and eating will probably be the preferred hand throughout life.

Attention span is also lengthening and your child may be able to sit quietly for up to 10 minutes while being read to or watching television. Stories and movies about daily life are usually the most likely to capture your child's attention for extended periods. Being able to identify with the children in the story is much more important than hearing about the strange adventures of make-believe characters.

Implications for swimming: Just as your toddler is beginning to show a preference for using either the left or right hand, your child is also beginning to prefer rolling to one side or the other when going from the front to the back position, or vice versa. The sooner you detect to which side the child naturally rolls, the less likely you are to confuse the child by rolling to the side opposite his or her natural tendencies.

As preference for using one arm or leg is becoming more established, your child may develop muscles on one side of the body that are significantly stronger than those on the other side. If that is the case, your toddler's swimming and kicking might lead to movement in a circle, rather than forward. There is no need for alarm, but do encourage your child to pull or kick equally with both sides of the body. Move your toddler's arms and legs with equal force to show what you mean. This can be done when sitting on the steps or while swimming in both the front and back positions.

Just as your toddler is beginning to show a preference for using either the left or right hand, he is also beginning to prefer rolling to one side or the other. (29 to 32 months)

Parent's role: If your toddler has been in swimming lessons for a while, your child really doesn't need your assistance during most of the lesson. Most of the lesson now takes place in the shallow end, where your toddler feels more in control. If you are part of a class and your child has been with the same teacher for several lessons, your toddler knows what the classroom procedure is and what to expect. Your child is mature enough to sit quietly on the steps with the other children and listen to the instructions, wait for a turn, and after performing, be satisfied with the teacher's or your approval.

On the other hand, if this is your child's first class, the teacher may want you to stay or may recommend another class consisting only of beginning children your child's age.

33 to 36 Months

Physical characteristics: As your child approaches age 3, body proportions begin to resemble those of an adult as much as they do those of a newborn. Between the ages of 2 and 6, body fat is reduced by 50%. Sex differences in body composition also start to appear. Boys have more muscle and bone while girls have more fatty tissue. There are also sex differences in how the children move. Boys use more of their total body when they are physically active, while girls' movements tend to be more isolated.

Implications for swimming: As body proportions begin to resemble those of adults, your child's swimming movements will also look more mature and less like dog paddling. If you have a daughter, front or back floating is fairly easy for her due to the high percentage of body fat. On the other hand, if your child is a boy, floating will be more difficult because his body is denser and more inclined to sink. He will have to expend more energy to stay afloat than the girls in his class, so do not blame him if he does not seem to be catching on to the idea of floating.

Emotional characteristics: Body language is a reliable clue to how your child is really feeling. Even though the child may be fairly adept at verbally communicating major feelings, it's difficult for most children this age to use words to explain the subtleties of their feelings. Sometimes they do not even know exactly what their feelings are and an adult has to clarify them.

Your child should also be learning that it is all right to be angry with you. When your toddler is being troublesome, and you have to resort to discipline, the child may react to your anger by being angry at you. It's important for you to explain that you are angry about what your child did but that you still love your child as much as you ever did. Eventually, your child will learn that, just like you, he or she can be angry with you for being disciplined, but can still love you.

Implications for swimming: During a swimming lesson, there are numerous incidents that might make your child angry, just as there are numerous ones that make your child happy. It's easy for your child to become confused and identify the target for anger as the swimming lesson itself or another person, rather than the instigating incident. These incidents are perfect times to teach your child to identify exactly what has caused the anger and how to handle that anger constructively.

For example, if your child becomes angry because the teacher does not allow pool toys to be taken home, the child may say that he or she hates the teacher. In reality, the child really does like the teacher, but has difficulty identifying what exactly should be the target of the anger. Once the anger is discussed openly and accepted, and the reason for the anger is understood, the child will be ready to move on and the incident will be forgotten.

Social characteristics: Playmates are an important aspect of your child's daily life now. Together with one or two friends, your child may create simple make-believe scenarios. Usually the story centers around familiar themes, like playing house, going to the grocery store, or changing a flat tire. Role playing during these make-believe scenarios helps your child identify how to act and how to relate to other children.

Implications for swimming: For many children this age, swimming class is fun, because they get to play in the water and they have friends there. During free time they can role play and make believe in ways we adults are too sophisticated to understand. The friendships built during class often extend to lunch or snack afterwards, or playing at each other's homes.

Intellectual characteristics: The ability to remember is becoming quite refined. Your toddler can remember past experiences and describe them in detailed sequence. The child can tell you what happened yesterday and what he or she wants to do tomorrow. No longer is your baby's world confined to the present.

Your child's memory functions so well on its own that it's easy to take it for granted. However, without too much effort, you can improve your son's or daughter's ability to remember by focusing on it during daily conversations. For example, you can ask your child what was eaten for breakfast or what color his or her coat is. By consciously prompting your child to think about those events that should be remembered, the likelihood they will be remembered is increased. Furthermore, the more your child knows what is going to happen the more secure your child will be.

Implications for swimming: From one lesson to the next, your child can remember skill sequences, the routine, and proper behavior during lessons. The more frequently during the week you and your child focus on these aspects of swimming lessons, the more likely your child will remember what to do. It's comforting for your child to know what's going to happen.

It's important for you to help your child remember the swimming lesson routine; it's also important for you to remember your routine before and after lessons. At this age, most children are very attached to that routine. If your toddler normally sits on the right side of the car on the way to swimming, the child may get very upset if switched to the left side. If you normally place your child's towel on a bench near the pool, but forget and place it in the locker room, your child may be magically transformed from a compliant angel to an uncooperative devil.

Of course, you should not be so concerned with maintaining a strict routine that the daily schedule is never varied; that only teaches your child to be inflexible. On the other hand, constant change is disruptive, and children do learn better if their environment is ordered. Swimming lessons will be more effective if you do maintain some type of routine.

Parent's role: At this age, children often become confused if more than one authority is teaching the class. When your child was younger, it was all right to be in a class where both you and the teacher were present; it was clear that you were in charge and that the teacher was just an interested bystander.

Now, as the teacher begins to take over instruction, your baby probably would function better with just one authority. It's time for your child to be in a class without you. Even staying to watch your child can be upsetting, as the child will be torn between looking to you for your reaction and listening to the teacher.

Moms and Dads often feel sad about giving up baby swimming classes with their child. For many parents, the most focused and fun time they spent with their baby was during those times. Clinging to those times and reenrolling in more parent/child swimming classes only holds your child back. You will be better off finding another joint activity to share with your youngster.

If you took lots of pictures, you and your child can relive those happy times and accomplishments. You can still share discussions with your child both before and after class. What is even more exciting is to go swimming just for the fun of it, without any teachers or other children to interfere with your relationship.

It's time for your child to be in a class without you. (33 to 36 months)

5
Chapter

Before Taking the Plunge

Trouble at your first formal swim lesson often begins in the locker room. A little preplanning can help ensure a pleasant swimming experience for you and your child.

Come Prepared

Trouble at the first formal swimming lesson is more likely to arise from improper preparation than from the actual water encounter. Parents, accustomed to the pool environment and procedure, take a visit to the pool for granted. Bringing a baby along, however, alters the situation. To prevent any unforeseen snags from turning into catastrophes, come prepared.

Pack Your Bag With These Essentials

1. Parent's swimsuit
2. Baby's swimsuit
3. Accessories to tie back parent's and baby's hair
4. Three towels
5. Baby's snack

6. Hand lotion
7. Diapering needs
8. Baby's favorite water-resistant toy

Arrive Early

By allowing time to investigate the pool environment before actually getting into the water, you can reduce your baby's anxiety about being in a strange, new place.

Come Relaxed and Thinking Positive

Babies are sensitive to their parents' body language. The more relaxed and confident you are, the more calm and secure your baby will feel, and the more successful the lessons will be.

Dress Comfortably

Choose a comfortable suit for yourself. Before your first lesson, familiarize your baby with your appearance in the suit, hat, sunglasses, and sunscreen you wear. It's no wonder some babies cry and squirm at seeing their parents in strange costumes!

Swimsuits and shorts are all appropriate choices for baby's swimwear. Just be sure they are not too tight or made of an absorbent fabric that will drag your baby down in the water. If you have a choice between a one-piece suit and a two-piece, opt for the one-piece as it will be more comfortable and less troublesome. Choose a suit with snug legs to catch unpredicted bowel movements. Bowel movements are rare, but if one occurs you will be much less embarrassed if most of the matter stays inside the suit. For this reason, nude bathing is not recommended.

Diapers, though, are not the answer. Both cloth and paper diapers become so saturated with water that they restrict babies' movements. Even worse is the tendency of paper diapers to disintegrate in the water, leaving a trail of tissue bits floating behind. Diapers do not keep urine and fecal matter out of the pool anyway. Urine quickly finds its way through diapers and into the pool where it is neutralized by pool chemicals. Fecal matter also escapes into the water, but swimsuits with snug legs contain it better than diapers. When a bowel movement does occur, parents are usually aware of it and quickly remove their baby from the pool. The small amount of fecal matter that does escape is quickly filtered out of the water. A few pools require diapers. Some even insist on double diapers covered by plastic pants. Check before the lesson to see what your pool requires.

Feed Your Baby a Light Snack

A light snack such as a cracker or piece of banana 15 minutes before the lesson can alleviate hunger without causing any difficulties for your child. A snack after the lesson also soothes hungry tummies and helps keep babies quiet while Mom or Dad dresses.

Schedule a Nap Before the Lesson

Rested and alert is how your baby should begin the class. A tired baby needs a warm, cozy place to sleep, and the pool is a poor substitute. Learning to swim is exhausting, and your baby needs to be rested to be active and happy throughout the lesson. Your baby will probably take a long nap after the lesson, too.

Introduce Yourself to the Rest of the Class

Making friends with the other parents and babies adds a delightful camaraderie to the lessons and capitalizes on your baby's natural tendency to learn by imitation. If your baby is busy touching and babbling with playmates, there is little room left for worry and boredom. Observing the others in the class laughing and playing water games will inspire your newcomer to join in, too.

Make the Proper Entrance

Babies who have not yet learned how to walk will have to be carried into the pool. The best way to enter the pool is by the steps. By steps we mean the wide, concrete kind built into the side of the pool, not the metal ladders hanging down into the water. Metal ladders are notoriously treacherous. They often are wobbly and slippery. With a baby in your arms, such ladders can be a real hazard. It's best to ignore ladders and proceed to the shallow end of the pool to the concrete steps. Position your baby at your side and step carefully into the pool.

Side Entrance—Unassisted

If steps are not available, sit on the edge of the pool and set your baby next to you. With one arm between the pool and your baby, turn toward the child and slide smoothly into the water. Once you are in the pool, you can safely bring your baby in with you.

With one arm between the pool and your baby, turn toward the child and slide smoothly into the water.

Side Entrance—Assisted

An easier side entrance, especially if your baby doesn't mind being touched by another adult, is for the teacher to steady the child while you slip into the water. Then, you can bring your baby in yourself.

Do Not Jump Into the Water

A jumping entrance is never a good idea. The noisy splash is frightening not only to your baby, but to the others in the class. Jumping also forces water up the baby's nose, increases the likelihood of falling, and may result in grazing you or your child's body against the side. A jumping entrance also encourages your baby to cling tightly to you, which inhibits the relaxation needed for proper learning.

Talk Soothingly

Whichever method you choose, the entrance will have a better chance of being tear-free if you talk reassuringly to your baby. Maintaining eye contact with your child also has a calming influence.

Lay a Firm Foundation

The following tips can provide the basis for one enjoyable experience after another.

Submerge to Shoulder Level

Babies held high out of the water get chilled quickly. Not only is the air temperature often cooler than the water, but also the evaporation of water from their skin draws off body heat.

Watch Your Baby's Face

During swimming lessons, your baby's head will be closer to the water than yours. If you are distracted, you may inadvertently let your baby's face drop below the surface. Such an unplanned dunking can be avoided if you always watch your child's face. Watching your baby's face also helps you keep better track of the child's moment to moment reactions so you can respond quickly and appropriately to changing needs.

Keep Moving

Babies need to associate being in the water with movement. This association is important not only in teaching them to move their arms and legs to stay afloat, but also in generating body heat to keep warm. Unless you are both active in the water, you will get cold.

Give the Eager Child Freedom

Eager children whose movements are overly restricted usually become frustrated. They need enough free movement to match their energy level. Although trying to hold an eager baby is like trying to hold a slippery eel, the parent must maintain control while permitting the child a large range of movement. If you are blessed with such an active baby, use a solid hold in conjunction with a soft, nonrestrictive touch. Avoid a tight hold, which is uncomfortable for both you and your baby and conveys a stressful, worried attitude. You will have to experiment to find the most efficient way of controlling your baby.

Be Imaginative

Guard against being overcautious. Too often parents worry that a little bit of water on their child's face will result in choking or drowning. More likely, the child will become bored and fussy from a lack of excitement and challenge. Be adventuresome, stimulate your child's imagination, and play games.

Allow the Cautious Child Time

Cautious babies need patient parents who readily provide them with extra time to adjust to the pool. Hurrying babies like this into learning swimming skills is a step in the wrong direction at high speed. Given time, these children will learn everything they need to know. If your baby fits into this category, the child will probably respond well to being held firmly and being allowed to carry a pacifier or other security object.

Assess the Pros and Cons of Handing Your Baby to a Stranger

Each baby is unique in the way he or she adjusts to the other adults in the class, and this adjustment may vary within the same child, depending on stage of development or mood. Newborns usually adjust well to strangers, but during the next 4 years, they often switch between accepting strangers and fearing them.

Throughout the lessons, at times you will be requested to hand your baby to other adults in the class. Since babies are capricious in their moods and their willingness to swim to others, it's usually worth a try to hand them over, even though you assume your baby will protest. You may be surprised to find your baby doesn't mind the switch at all.

Several good reasons exist for giving your child experience in going to other adults. For one, the teacher has more experience and skill in handling babies in the water and may wish to demonstrate a particular technique for you. Also, some babies have such a strict definition of what they perceive their parents should do that they are reluctant to allow their parents to try something new, such as teaching them to swim. If such is the case with your baby, the child may readily perform for the teacher, but not for you. Some skills are actually less frightening if another adult is involved, such as swimming from one person to another. Your baby may be much happier swimming to you from another adult than swimming from you. Your child must also discover that other adults can teach as well as you. Starting young usually makes this discovery easier in the long run and the separation process from you less anxiety-ridden.

However, at certain times in your baby's life, it's better to refrain from handing your baby to a stranger. Perhaps your child is not feeling well or is tired. Perhaps your child is at the peak of a "clinging stage." Perhaps there is a real personality clash between your baby and the other adult. In any of these situations, handing your child to another adult will only produce tears and anger, which prevent further learning. If you force the issue, nothing is gained but a determination in your baby to avoid similar situations in the future.

Be Sensitive to Your Baby's Crying

Crying is the way your baby communicates with you. There are many reasons why your baby cries, but being in the water is one of the least likely. If you get out of the pool every time your baby cries, the child will begin to associate being in the water with crying. Then, whenever you get in the pool, your baby will be conditioned to respond by crying. If your baby does cry when you are in the water, instead of getting out, try to determine the real cause of your baby's tears. The Crying Troubleshooter (Table 1) will help you determine the reason for your baby's crying and how to stop it.

Make the Proper Exit

As with entering the water, getting out is easy if the pool has steps. Don't climb up the metal ladders that hang down the side of the pool, though. Trying to climb up the wobbly, slippery, narrow steps on such a ladder, one-handed, and holding a wet baby with the other hand can lead to a nasty fall.

Side Exit—Assisted

If the pool does not have steps, ask the teacher or a friend to hold your baby while you climb out.

Side Exit—Unassisted

If there are no steps and no one is available to hold your baby, sit or lay your baby on the deck on the pool near the edge. With one arm between your baby and the pool, lift yourself out. While climbing out, keep a close watch on your child, as energetic tots find it great fun to jump back in the water or to crawl or run away.

Table 1 Crying Troubleshooter

Cause/Symptoms	Solutions
COLD WATER Blue fingernails, lips; goosebumps, shivering (does not always occur)	Dress baby in long sleeved shirt; submerge child to neck level; or leave the water. If water is always cold, find a pool with warm water.
FATIGUE Yawning; child rests head on your shoulder; reluctant to play	Hold child close to you; spend rest of time walking around, talking, watching other babies, or go home. Reschedule nap time.
HUNGER Sucking on fist; child chews on your shoulder	Light snack before lesson; offer breast or bottle during lesson. No heavy meals before or during lesson.
UNDERSTIMULATION/BOREDOM Baby shows no interest in class activities	Give baby a toy; play silly games.
OVERSTIMULATION Baby turns away from class; rejects play; refuses to learn new skill; seems overwhelmed	Allow child some quiet time; slow pace so child can internalize skills already taught; step back away from the class for a few minutes.
NOISE Sudden noise; high-pitched wavering voices in the pool area	Use soft, low, steady voice; ask others to lower voices.
PARENTAL ANXIETY Frustrated, worried, distracted, tense parent teamed with child who has the same symptoms	Try to erase worried feelings; concentrate on having a pleasant time; take slow deep breaths; hold baby loosely at your hip; relax your jaw, smile, talk cheerfully.
MORO REFLEX Child detects loss of balance or support and flings arms out to break fall	Provide lots of body contact and support; hold child's hands close to the body during maneuvers, especially when lying back in water.

With one arm between your baby and the pool, lift yourself out.

Leave the Pool Before Your Baby Gets Fussy

If the water is warm, babies usually can stay in for 30 minutes. It's tempting to remain longer, especially if your baby is having fun, but leaving while the child is happy insures that the lessons will be remembered as enjoyable.

Take Off Your Baby's Swimsuit in the Water

Take your baby's swimsuit off before wrapping the child in a towel. If the air temperature is cool, consider taking off the suit while still in the water. Not only will the suit slide off easier, since the water acts as a lubricant, but the time your baby is exposed to the cooling effects of the air is shortened.

Wrap Your Baby in a Towel

Place a towel near the pool before the lesson so that it will be immediately available to wrap around your baby when the lesson is finished. When you get to the dressing room, lay your warm bundle on a soft towel on the floor or in an infant seat. Your baby will stay warm and dry while you dress.

Have a Snack Ready

Your baby will probably be hungry after swimming, so have a bottle, a breast, or finger food readily available. If your child is eating, you can dress uninterrupted.

Dress Yourself First

Although you may feel selfish dressing yourself first, it is actually the most caring procedure. If you dress your baby first, your wet swimsuit will drip on the child's dry clothes. An even soggier situation unfolds when your baby crawls through the puddles on the locker room floor.

There are times when your baby should be dressed first. If your baby is exposed to windy or cool weather, the child should be dressed first. Just make sure you put your baby in a dry place.

Schedule a Nap After the Lesson

Parents frequently comment on how much they like swimming lessons because their babies sleep so well afterward. If you need free time, take your baby swimming. After the lesson, you can be pretty sure of having several undisturbed hours while your baby sleeps.

6
Chapter

The Eight Basic Skills

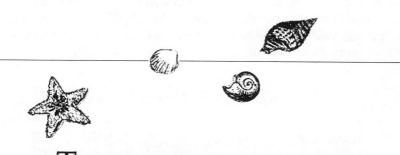

The lessons revolve around eight basic skills. Teach these skills to your own baby by following the step-by-step instructions. Discover the keys to success, how to handle common problems, and how to adjust for your baby's personality.

A good baby swim class must do four things: teach the eight basic skills, adapt to individual personalities, adjust for developmental differences (chapters 3 and 4), and be managed efficiently (chapter 7). In this chapter you will learn how to teach the eight basic skills and how to adapt these skills to three personality types: eager, cautious, and typical. The general instructions address the needs of typical babies, whereas the needs of eager and cautious babies are handled in separate sections.

All eight basic skills can be practiced by all age groups, as long as teaching techniques are modified to match each age group's developmental level. Although a few suggestions as to how to adapt each skill to different ages are included in this chapter under Keys to Success, most considerations relating to developmental differences are addressed in chapter 4. Chapter 7 explains how lessons can be modified to meet the needs of newborns (0 to 6 months), babies (6 to 15 months), toddlers (15 months to 3 years), and independent toddlers (2-1/2 to 3-1/2 years).

The key points of each skill are summarized in the section called "The Bottom Line."

If you and your spouse or a friend are teaching your baby without the assistance of an instructor, this chapter provides all the "how-to" information you need to know from the first lesson up to the time your baby learns how to swim several yards independent of your support. If you are teaching your baby with an instructor, this chapter will help you become better informed so you will be a more effective parent/child pair. The more knowledgeable you are, the less anxious you will be, and the more likely your baby will be happy and self-confident.

Stomach Position

Figure 1   Enjoy success in the first lesson by choosing the stomach position that best matches your baby's development. Method A works well with very young babies who need help holding up their heads. Use your palms to support your baby's chest, while your fingers point toward the child's toes and your thumbs wrap around the child's upper arms.

Figure 2   Older babies need less support and more freedom than Method A allows. Method B usually works better for them. Hold your baby under the arm pits, your fingers pointing toward the child's back. Your thumb position may vary from around the child's shoulder to under the chest.

Figure 3   Confident, experienced babies need more freedom of movement than either Methods A or B provide. Method C fits their needs best. Hold your baby at your side with your arm encircling your baby's back and the finger-tips of the other hand pointing toward the child's chest.

Figure 4   Oops! Trying to change from either Method A or B to C without moving your hands is possible if you are a contortionist. But, it's much easier to switch hands whenever you move your baby into the side position (Method C).

Figure 5   Standing still while holding your baby in the stomach position is boring. Instead, take advantage of water currents by walking backwards. The water displaced by your body will surge upward and under your baby to help keep the child afloat.

Figure 6   Half of your baby's body should be underwater. This permits your baby to feel the buoyancy of the water and allows you to relax your grip. Your baby will be warmer in this position and actually feel more secure, as both your hands and the water are giving support.

Figure 7   Babies held too high out of the water feel uncomfortable, cold, and insecure. Holding your baby low in the water is better.

Figure 8 Another distracted parent! Practically every baby experiences a surprise face full of water because Mom or Dad is distracted and accidentally allows the baby's face to dip under the surface.

Figure 9 Water tickling your baby's chin can be delightful! As early as the first lesson, your baby can enjoy chin level water. A baby will rarely choke in this position, even if the water briefly covers his or her mouth.

Figure 10 Boisterous, active babies are often bored in the stomach position. If your baby needs a little excitement, try some gentle splashing, swishing through the water, and playing with toys.

Figure 11 "Travel" can also stave off boredom, so explore new territory with your baby. Some of the more interesting pool sights are the skimmer holes and cold or warm water returns.

Figure 12 Teething babies may need help relaxing. Chewing on soft toys frequently works. But don't let your child become too dependent on them. Your baby needs free hands to swim.

Keys to Success

1. To prevent accidental dunking and give your baby added security, face your child and maintain eye contact.
2. Stand in midriff level water. It's the depth that's most conducive to holding your baby in the proper position.
3. Your hands convey nonverbal messages to your baby, so use them lovingly.
4. Maintain a gentle, calm voice, no matter what happens.

5. Once you are comfortable with the basic hold, add variations such as swishing your baby from side to side, playing with toys, and exploring the pool.

6. By extending your arms and rotating your wrists, you position your baby in a more horizontal position. The closer to your body you hold your baby (excluding the side position), the more vertical the child's position.

7. Remember that nonstrenuous classes produce almost as much fitness as do more rigorous ones, at least in babies. The reason for this is not clear, but one theory explains it this way. Certain hormones not present in the human body until after puberty determine the maximum fitness level an individual can expect from physical training. Because babies have low levels of these hormones, rigorous training has little effect on fitness. Parents of baby swimmers should concentrate on teaching basic skills and enjoyment of the water, rather than endurance training. Until puberty, most of the effort that goes into rigorous training is wasted.

Eager Personality

If your baby is the type that throws caution to the winds and tries to wriggle out of your arms, maintain firm, gentle pressure with your hands so that the child doesn't lunge free of your control. Such eager babies may get bored with this basic position, unless you provide extra excitement by playing games.

Cautious Personality

A cautious and hesitant baby will probably be happiest if allowed to progress in an unrushed manner. Also, try holding the child closer to you in a more vertical position.

This type of baby generates little body heat through movement and, consequently, gets cold quickly. If your child falls into this category, try dressing your baby in a shirt and be sure to keep the child's body under the water's surface at all times.

The Bottom Line

1. Experiment with the three different stomach positions until you find the one that works best for your baby.
2. Control the degree of your baby's horizontalness by extending your arms and rotating your wrists.
3. Walk backward while facing your baby. If your child is in the side position, walk forward.
4. Keep at least half of your baby's body underwater.

Back Position

Figure 1   Emotional security is the key to success in teaching babies the back position. The more physical contact between you and your baby, the more secure your baby usually feels. For the greatest sense of security, lay your baby's head on your shoulder and gently place your cheek on the child's head.

Figure 2   Eventually, your baby will begin to relax and trust that you will not let him or her fall while lying back. Gradually reduce physical contact until you are supporting the child's body (one hand under the back, the other hand under the head) against your chest.

Figure 3   "Let me do it myself," your baby demands while becoming more independent. To give your child this freedom while you still maintain control, support the child's head with one hand and bottom with the other.

Figure 4   In all back positions, the level of the water should reach just above your baby's ears. This permits the child to feel the buoyancy of the supporting water. It is also less distracting to the child if the water level remains constant instead of varying above and below ear level.

Figure 5 Eye contact and a soothing voice have an almost magical effect in relaxing your baby. Moreover, as the child relaxes and looks back at your face, your baby naturally extends the neck, which helps align the body in the correct floating position.

Figure 6 Walking backwards creates a current around your body that helps keep your baby afloat.

Figure 7   Trying to sit up while in the back position is a natural reaction for most babies. Frustrated parents may blame their baby's stubbornness, but the real culprit is most likely the righting reflex. The righting reflex causes your baby to try to keep the head upright whenever the brain senses the body is falling. If your baby continually tries to sit up, do not force your child to lie back.

Figure 8   If your baby continually tries to sit up or cries, try holding the child in a semisitting cradle position. This provides the added security of being close to you while at the same time allowing you to keep the child low in the water. Giving the child a toy also helps.

Figure 9   Emily's favorite way of relaxing (breast or bottle feeding).

Figure 10   Sunny days in outdoor pools can be a problem. Babies dislike lying on their backs when the sun blinds their eyes. If you are faced with this problem, shield your baby's eyes with your hand, head, or hat.

Figure 11   The great foot discovery! Around age 5 months, toe chewing be-comes a favorite pastime. As long as the child is relaxed and the water level is above the ears, there is no harm in toe play. With maturity, this behavior will disappear.

Figure 12   Young babies prefer to keep their arms folded close to their bodies.

Figure 13   If your baby is very relaxed and needs little support in the back position, then your child is ready for a more advanced back float. Place your hands under or at the sides of your child's head. To maintain correct body position, talk as your child looks straight up into your face.

Figure 14   While walking backwards, gradually ease your fingers away until the child is floating alone. Keep a hand close by in case your baby's head starts to sink.

Figure 15   Fat has its advantages—it weighs less than bone or muscle. For this reason, thin babies have more trouble learning to float than fatter ones. Lucky Kevin! He has just enough fat to make floating a dream.

Keys to Success

1. Survival is one reason your baby needs to become accustomed to lying back in the water. A child who falls into the water can breathe most easily by rolling onto the back and waiting for help to arrive. Most babies cannot do this unaided until they are at least 2 or 3 years old, but all babies can learn to back float with support.

2. Your baby will have reasons for either loving or hating the back position. It's important that you tune yourself in to your own child's feelings on the subject. If your baby does not

relish lying back in the water, the reasons listed below may help you understand why.

- The water feels strange in your baby's ears.
- Your child's eyes have nothing on which to focus, causing an unsteady feeling.
- The righting reflex, which operates whenever a baby feels he or she is losing balance, causes the child to try to sit up or roll over in an attempt to keep the head upright.
- When your child can't see you, he or she may feel insecure.
- If a toddler, your child probably enjoys being independent of you and controlling the environment. When in the back position, your child becomes dependent on you once again, and that may cause frustration.

3. Your baby will adapt to the back position more readily after having had happy back experiences in the bathtub.
4. If your child is less than 8 months old, you can minimize the risk of crying as a result of the Moro reflex by securely supporting both the child's head and body. Folding your baby's arms across the chest also helps.
5. Don't be surprised if your baby's legs raise perpendicularly into the air. To relax the child's legs, maintain calming eye contact, talk soothingly, provide a toy, or gently lay your hand on the child's thighs.
6. Water wings, small air-filled pillows that attach to your baby's upper arms, can help your child make the transition from a supported back float to an independent back float. Most babies younger than 18 months don't like water wings, and even older children may find them confining. If your child enjoys them, initially use them fully inflated as you support your child in the back position. Gradually, over at least 10 lessons, inflate them less and less as you simultaneously begin to remove your hand support. Eventually your child may be able to float alone. Don't force them on your child, though. Children who don't use water wings usually learn to back float more quickly than those who do.

Eager Personality

A minority of children seem to delight in the back position and enjoy the calming, gurgling sounds of water in their ears. These babies relax quite easily on their backs and need very little support. No matter how naturally they seem to back float, however, most babies' heads tend to sink, and parents should keep a supportive hand ready to nudge their child's head a little higher whenever necessary.

It's often the children who have calm personalities who are most eager to back float. Energetic babies tend to splash and kick while on their backs, which causes them to sink. These children need to be watched carefully, as they often arch backward or roll to the side, dunking their heads underwater. These submersions plus their natural inability to relax and stop moving are big factors in why very active babies have difficulty adapting to the back position.

Cautious Personality

Apprehension in the back position is the rule rather than the exception. Babies who continue to cry for more than 10 seconds are obviously very distressed and should not be forced to remain on their backs very long. The semisitting position (Figure 8) is usually more agreeable to them. Gradually, they can be reintroduced to the standard back positions (Figures 1, 2, 3).

The Bottom Line

1. For your baby's first attempt, choose a back position that provides lots of physical contact.
2. Keep the water level just above your baby's ears.
3. Maintain eye contact and talk soothingly.
4. Walk backward.

Kicking

Figure 1   Kicking does not come naturally to all babies. More than likely your child will have to be shown. For your first attempt, stand in shoulder-deep water, holding your baby under the arms, while another person moves the child's legs reciprocally (alternately) up and down.

Figure 2   Alas! You're the only one available to do the four-handed job of both holding your baby and moving the child's legs. With only two hands available, the easiest way of doing this is to put your baby's arms on your shoulders, while using your hands to manipulate the child's legs.

Figure 3 Kevin, like other babies with lots of swimming experience, does not need the extra security of being held close. With an outstretched arm, his teacher supports his upper arm (the one farthest away) with one hand while manipulating his legs with the other. Kevin's chin and free hand rest on his teacher's outstretched arm.

Figure 4 One amazing day you discover that your baby has learned to associate the word "kick" with its meaning and you no longer need to move the child's legs. At this point, hold your baby facing you with your fingers supporting the child's chest and your thumbs wrapped over the back. Say "kick, kick, kick."

Figure 5 Kicking on the back and stomach can be introduced at the same time. For back kicking, lay your baby's head on your shoulder and support the child's back with your upper arm. Move your baby's legs reciprocally up and down.

Figure 6 Kevin has built up enough confidence so his teacher needs only to support his head.

Figure 7 Different babies kick different ways and at different speeds. It doesn't matter how your baby kicks, only that your child learns to associate the word "kick" with leg movement. One of the most common baby kicks resembles the leg motion used for riding a bicycle.

Figure 8 It may look funny, but the frog kick is a legitimate baby kick. If your baby bends both legs and extends them in unison, consider yourself the parent of a "frog kicker."

Figure 9 Your baby may even be a one-legged kicker. Although it is not efficient, it is acceptable. Children are generally not capable of consciously refining their kicks until they are at least 2-1/2 years old.

Figure 10 Lightly stroking the bottoms of your baby's feet is another way of getting a nonkicker to move the legs.

Figure 11   Babies, especially those who are crawling, sometimes can be coaxed into kicking by placing a toy just out of reach. Daddies are great attractions, too!

Keys to Success

1. Always say "kick, kick, kick" whenever you want your baby to kick, even if you are moving the child's legs.
2. Your baby will associate the word "kick" with its meaning sooner, if you practice at home, both in and out of the water. During diaper changes and other spare moments, say "kick, kick, kick" and move your baby's legs in reciprocal motion.
3. Don't get discouraged. It's not unusual for babies to take 10 classes or more before they start kicking on their own. Some babies are so calm and relaxed in the water that they simply have no desire to move their legs. Others are so tense they can't move their legs at all.

4. Nonkickers are also a common type. If your child is one, try stimulating leg movement by holding your baby on the stomach while another adult stretches out the child's leg, until your baby resists by flexing the leg and bringing it back close to the body.

Eager Personality

Active babies who play and splash in the water will probably start kicking during their first lesson. Staying in one place is not their style, and their eager kicking is a way of saying "Let's get going." If your baby is wound up like this, you need to get going, too. As your baby kicks, move around the pool. Even though kicking is too inefficient for self-propulsion, your child needs to feel that kicking produces movement.

Cautious Personality

Babies who are worried in the water may take a long time to start kicking. Their tenseness keeps their leg muscles tight and inhibits them in alternately relaxing and contracting the muscles needed for kicking. Forcing these babies to kick before they are ready only leads to more tension, which tightens up their kick even more.

If your child is very tense, don't concentrate on kicking. Instead, emphasize playing whatever games your child likes. As your baby begins to enjoy the water, your child will begin to relax enough for the leg muscles to kick freely.

The Bottom Line

1. Experiment with the four kicking positions on the stomach and the two on the back until you find the ones that work best for your baby.
2. Move your baby's legs in reciprocal kicking motion until your baby starts kicking alone.
3. Say "kick, kick, kick" whenever you want your baby to kick.

Pulling

Figure 1 Pulling refers to the arm movement babies use to propel themselves through the water. For babies, it is not a very efficient way of self-propulsion. It is a very important skill for your baby to master, though, as pulling eventually will become your child's strongest means of propulsion.

Figure 2 With luck, the pool will have a step deep enough so that you can sit on it waist deep with your child in your lap. As you hold your baby and say ''pull, pull, pull,'' demonstrate the action by moving the baby's arms. The child's first attempt may look like splashing.

Figure 3 If your baby is old enough to sit alone, set your child on the step and use your hands to manipulate the arms in reciprocal pulling motion.

Figure 4 If your baby cannot sit alone and if the pool doesn't have an underwater step to sit on, you will have the wobbly job of moving your baby's arms while standing. Lean against the side of the pool and bend your knee to make a seat. Steady your baby on your knee with your upper arms, and use your hands to move the child's arms.

Figure 5 "Let me do it myself!" This is what we hope eventually happens. Place your child on his stomach facing you, and back away, encouraging the baby to pull.

Figure 6 Does your baby crave excitement and find pulling a wee bit boring? Then, forget about keeping yourself comfortably dry and teach your child to splash. Start by gently splashing your baby's hands. Before long, the child will be splashing gleefully alone. For some babies, splashing is the key to unlocking their tightly folded arms.

Keys to Success

1. Before age 2, the shortness of your baby's arms and the instinctive reaction to hold them close to the body prevent pulling from being effective for propulsion.
2. Babies often cry when their arms are unfolded, so don't force your child's arms open if it causes the child to cry. Wait for the child to calm down before trying again.
3. Learning to extend their arms is a slow process for most babies. Initially their arm pulling movement is practically imperceptible. Only with maturation will your baby become capable of full arm extension.
4. Although your baby may resist arm extension, you might be able to trick your baby into it. Place a favorite item, such as yourself or a toy, just out of your baby's reach and encourage the child to get it. Often the child will begin pulling in an attempt to reach the object. When trying this trick, though, be careful not to move your baby toward the object until pulling begins.
5. Effective pulling usually takes longer to learn than kicking. Be patient and don't worry if your baby isn't progressing as quickly as you think is appropriate.
6. Always say "pull, pull, pull" during arm movement.
7. The only place pulling is effective is underwater. Splashing is a fun warm-up game, but be sure to follow it with some underwater pulling practice by holding your baby's shoulders under the surface.
8. Encourage your baby's arm extension at home by placing the child's toys just out of reach.
9. Pulling experience could save your baby from drowning. A child who has no experience pulling to the side may fall into

the water and may not realize that by extending the arms he or she could hang onto the edge to get a breath. Instead, such a child might wait passively in the water until either it drowns or help arrives.

10. Like a turtle, your baby will progress slowly. Eventually, the child will be able to pull alone. Then you can graduate to holding your baby at your side and simply telling the child to pull.

Eager Personality

Eager babies often interpret pulling as splashing. This is fine as long as they are kept away from babies who are frightened by such boisterousness. Splashing can be overdone, though, so these babies need to be encouraged to transfer the energy that goes into top of the water splashing to underwater pulling. All of that splashing above the surface is wasted effort as far as propulsion is concerned.

Cautious Personality

The instinct to keep their arms close to their bodies is strongest in babies less than a year old, but even older children who are tense in the water may hold their arms tight. If this is the case with your child, you may find it impossible to pry the arms away from the child's sides.

Since force usually only brings stubborn screams, you may have to content yourself with holding the child's hands and moving them ever so slightly up and down. The kinesthetic stimulation within the child's muscles, though minor, is sufficient for the child to begin to associate arm movement with the word "pull."

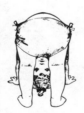

The Bottom Line

1. Sit in the water with your baby facing away from you. If another person is available to help, he or she can move the child's arms in an alternate pulling fashion.
2. If another person is not available, sit on the step or stand against the side and move the baby's arms yourself.
3. Always say "pull, pull, pull" during arm movement.
4. Hold your baby at your side in the prone position to encourage pulling without adult help.

Submerging

Figure 1   Surprisingly, submerging is one of the easiest learned skills. Before trying a total submersion, though, practice gently swishing your baby through the water at chin level, using a basic stomach position.

Figure 2   After your baby is comfortable with chin level water, try a mini-dunk. Simply hold your baby in the stomach position and allow the water to wash over the child's mouth, then nose, and finally eyes.

Figure 3   Babies' faces need to be watched closely so that their mouths and noses aren't submerged before they are ready. Submersion should not occur until your baby is aware that going underwater is imminent. It's imperative to get your child's attention before starting.

Figure 4   Closing is usually obvious, being accompanied by a scrunched-up nose, tightly closed eyes, and various other signs unique to each baby.

Figure 5 Choking during submersion is less likely if you give your baby cues before going underwater. We always begin with the verbal cue, "1, 2, 3," followed by the kinesthetic cue of lifting the child a few inches.

Figure 6 Lower your baby's face into the water only after the child has "closed" (stopped breathing).

Figure 7   As soon as closing is complete, calmly submerge your baby's face. It's that easy!

Figure 8   Smoothly bring your baby out of the water and celebrate the submersion with a big hug and smiling praise. Be sure you do not give your baby the impression he or she has just been rescued from a horrible fate.

Figure 9   As the baby gains confidence, gradually lengthen the amount of time spent underwater.

Figure 10   Submersions that start by setting your baby on the side of the pool are a fun variation. We usually sing the Humpty Dumpty rhyme as the initial cue, bringing the baby into the water on ''had a great fall.''

Figure 11 By using several cues together, the chance of alerting your baby to the submersion is increased. If your child frequently forgets to close, try adding the cue of blowing softly into your child's face. Blowing causes instinctive closure of both eyes and nose, but we advise its use only when necessary.

Figure 12 During first submersions, babies may come up with a surprised or confused look. Do not interpret this as an indication of discomfort. After several successful submersions, babies usually come up smiling—especially if their parents flash them a grin first.

Keys to Success

1. If your child continually cries or balks at submersion, don't force the issue. Wait for several lessons to pass before trying again.
2. Approach submersion with a positive outlook. Babies who never have the opportunity to experience submersion may never learn the importance of holding their breath and controlling their breathing while underwater. These are skills that must be mastered for water survival.
3. If you carefully observe your baby's face for closure, chances are your child won't breathe in water. However, a child who has an allergy or a cold may attempt to breathe underwater, even after closure.
4. The correct submersion position is more horizontal than vertical. If your baby is in a vertical position, water is likely to be forced up into the nose as you push your child down through the water.
5. The entire submersion process, from cues through the final hug, should be one, continuous, smooth movement. Don't jerk your child under and quickly back up in an attempt to reduce your baby's time underwater. It only alarms your baby and sets off the Moro reflex, causing the child to inhale and choke. Your child will then associate submersion with choking and may start crying whenever you give the cue for submersion.
6. Be consistent with the cues you give your baby before submersion. The cues described here are only suggestions. You may choose different cues as long as you use them consistently and in the same order before submersion.
7. The amount of time between cues and submersion is crucial. If the time is too short, babies will not have time to take

a breath and hold it. Short timing may also take them by surprise, which may cause them to gasp and suck in water. On the other hand, if the time between cues and submersion is too long, babies may not associate the cues with the submersion and consequently will not close in time for the submersion. Another hazard of long timing is that babies can hold their breath for only a short time.

8. Unless it is obvious that your baby has missed the cues and is not closed, don't stop between cues and submersion. By not following through, you are teaching your baby that breath holding need not always follow the cues. The result is a baby who doesn't learn to anticipate submersion and who inhales and chokes underwater.

9. The signs for closing vary from baby to baby. Some may be closed even if their eyes and mouth are open. Babies almost always breathe through the nose, and as long as the nose is closed, they usually do not take in water. To be sure babies who keep their eyes and mouth open are closed, listen carefully for them to inhale and feel the chest inflate as they stop breathing.

10. Do not treat choking as a major catastrophe. It isn't. Your baby won't think it is either, unless you overreact. Fortunately, nature has provided babies with a strong coughing reflex, and within a few seconds the tiny amount of water inhaled is expelled by coughing or sneezing. Your best response to choking is to calmly hold your baby until the coughing stops, then give a hug and proceed to a different activity.

11. While your child is underwater, watch for bubbles. They indicate that your child is exhaling and will soon have to inhale. If you see such bubbles, smoothly bring your baby to the surface.

12. Relax, relax, relax! Parents almost always fear submersion more than their children do. Submersion is not harmful when done correctly, and with practice most babies find it fun. Parental worry often manifests itself as a concerned look, tense hold, and avoidance of underwater skills, all negative cues that transmit your fear to your baby.

13. Don't put off submersion until your baby is older, rationalizing that older children can handle it better. Actually, younger children accept the underwater environment more quickly than do older ones. They have not yet learned to

fear water, and they trust you to take care of them. They learn to accept submersion just as easily as they accept a diaper change.

14. Swallowing occurs when babies take in water through their mouths and into their stomachs. This is not a problem unless large amounts are swallowed and the child becomes water intoxicated. To make sure your baby does not swallow a harmful amount, see the section on hyponatremia (water intoxication) in Appendix A.

15. Allow time to play between submersions. At first, two or three times going underwater per lesson is sufficient.

16. If your child has a minor head cold, remember that the high humidity around the pool helps clear stuffy noses, making breathing easier. If, however, your child's nasal passages remain clogged so that breathing is difficult, irregular, or through the mouth, submersion should be postponed until the next lesson.

17. With practice, most babies outgrow their need for cues. As soon as they detect that their face is approaching the water, they automatically hold their breath.

Eager Personality

While being swished through the water for minidunks, eager babies often find it fun to drop their faces in the water. This is great, as long as they are held high enough in the water to lift their heads out when they want.

This type of child usually loves submersion, but such babies have their limit too. Their giggles and smiles encourage their parents to submerge repeatedly. Such submersions are exhausting and as the babies tire, they lose control of their breathing and inevitably end up choking and crying. Exercise moderation in going underwater, even with babies who obviously love it.

Cautious Personality

Even though their babies are wary, parents must always follow the cues for submersion with going underwater. Procrastination only increases fear and anxiety. It is much healthier for your baby's psyche to follow through and complete the submersion. For cautious babies, one submersion per lesson is sufficient.

However, certain babies should never be submerged, particularly those who always sniff in water and never hold their breath. For these children, there may be a physiological reason, such as allergy or sinus problems, that interferes with their ability to hold their breath.

Whatever the reason, sniffing in water hurts. If the cause is physiological, submersion will have to be postponed until the breathing problem is resolved. If the cause is merely the child's personal reluctance to going underwater, try using "side" submersions or accentuating the cues. As a last resort, parents can hold their child's nose but only if their baby is agreeable to the procedure.

The Bottom Line

1. When you have your baby's attention, lift the child several inches and count ''1, 2, 3.''
2. Watch to see that your child is not inhaling.
3. Using one continuous movement, submerge your baby's face, then smoothly bring your child to the surface.
4. Greet your baby with a big smile and hug!

Swimming

Figure 1   A baby should be able to hold the breath 3 seconds before beginning to swim unassisted. Set the child on the side, count to 3, and gently pull your baby into the water.

Figure 2 When your baby is underwater, let go and allow the child to swim freely for a few seconds before picking your baby up. While the child is swimming, say ''kick and pull.''

Figure 3 After several successful swims, instead of picking your baby up, encourage the child to lift its head out of the water by extending your arm only. After seeing your arm, hopefully your baby will reach for it and pull up and out of the water for a breath.

Figure 4   The next step is to teach your baby to swim to the side of the pool. Hold your baby at your side and tilt the child's body downward. Gently shove the child toward the wall, saying "kick and pull."

Figure 5   If your baby is too young to grab the edge unassisted, lightly lift the child's bottom until he or she is high enough out of the water to grab the edge.

Figure 6   Place your hands over your child's hands to prevent them from slipping off the edge. With each successive swim move farther away from the wall.

Figure 7   While being pushed to the side, your baby may change course by turning around and swimming back to you. For safety's sake, stay out of the child's reach and gently steer your baby back toward the wall.

Figure 8 Besides swimming to the side, your baby also can swim between the teacher and you. The teacher holds your child in the side position, tilts your baby downward while counting to three, and pushes the child underwater to you, saying "kick and pull."

Figure 9 Keeping your baby's face down in the water is easier said than done. There are three tricks we use to accomplish this. The simplest and most effective way is to tilt the child slightly downward when beginning a swim. Bear in mind that keeping your baby's face down in the water does not mean forcing the child underwater when the child is reluctant. Many children willingly put their heads in the water, but not at the horizontal angle necessary for efficient swimming. These are the children who can benefit from these tricks.

Figure 10   A second trick is to hold a toy for the child to swim to just under the surface.

Figure 11   The third way involves pulling on the baby's head. Because this trick can backfire by making the baby push back against your hand pressure, we use it only as a last resort.

Figure 12 When your baby is swimming away from you, the pushing is a horizontal force, propelling the child forward.

Keys to Success

1. Swimming to the side is a skill that could save your child's life. Children have drowned within reach of the side, simply because they were never taught that by hanging onto the edge they could keep their heads above water until help arrived.
2. Don't be surprised if your baby's swimming resembles "dog paddling." Babies aren't capable of mastering an extended arm pull until they are older.
3. After becoming comfortable with the class, your baby will have fun swimming from one adult to another. The parents in the class can stand in a circle and pass each baby to the neighboring adult. The babies continue to be passed around

the circle until they are back with their own parent. Of course, if your baby gets impatient before finishing the complete circuit, your child can take a shortcut back to you.

4. Babies are usually more motivated to swim from teacher to parent. As they become familiar with the other adults, they learn to enjoy swimming to them also.

5. Be consistent in the time you allow your baby to stay under the water. Counting aloud the number of seconds your child is under helps your baby judge the amount of time needed for breath holding. As your baby becomes more proficient, gradually increase the number of seconds underwater.

6. To prevent choking, bring your baby to the surface before inhalation. The following signs indicate that your baby will soon be inhaling: a tense facial expression, air bubbles coming from your baby's mouth, and frantic arm and leg movement.

7. Remind your baby to kick and pull while swimming. If you loudly say ''kick and pull'' near the water's surface, your baby can hear you, even underwater.

8. To stimulate kicking and pulling, flick the bottoms of your baby's feet and the tips of your baby's fingers.

9. Eventually, as swimming distance increases, your baby may need an additional nudge on the back to reach the wall or other adult. Don't nudge too soon, though! That can rob your child of the thrill of accomplishing something all alone.

10. Never allow your baby to swim back to you once it has been pushed toward the wall. That only teaches the child that you will always be there to help. Consequently, your baby will never feel the need to become self-reliant in the water.

11. Initially, the distance should be short, and your hands should stay with your baby throughout the swim. As the distance increases, your hands should be withdrawn sooner, allowing the child a few seconds to swim unassisted.

12. Don't push your child more than several inches under the water when beginning a swim. Deep pushes are appropriate for learning to dive, but detract from learning to swim.

13. Swimming in a horizontal position does not come naturally. A vertical position prevents their kicking and pulling from effectively propelling them forward. To counteract this tendency in your baby, tilt the child's head downward

(remember head position controls body position). You also can try holding a brightly colored toy or your own face underwater for your child to look at while swimming.

14. Chin lifts can greatly boost your baby's confidence. Five or six chin lifts may be all your child needs to swim the width of the pool. This accomplishment may give your baby the courage to try it alone. See Breath Control, Figure 6.

15. No matter how short the swim, treat yourself and your baby to a delicious hug and grin. Cheer on the others in the class, too!

Eager Personality

Swimming is such a thrill for some babies that they eagerly jump off the side or lunge out of their parents' arms to get in the water. They are totally confident that help will arrive whenever they need it. But, someday they may plunge in when help isn't nearby and either drown or become so scared they develop aquaphobia.

To discourage this hazardous practice, we let such children stay underwater an extra second (never long enough for them to choke or for fear to set in) hoping they will realize that Mom or Dad may not always be ready to catch them. When we finally bring them to the surface, we emphasize the importance of waiting to jump until someone is ready to catch them.

Cautious Personality

If your baby is reluctant to separate from you and doesn't like being released in the water, try retaining physical contact with the child throughout the swim. With each subsequent swim, gradually reduce that contact until the child is swimming alone.

If your baby doesn't like swimming because of being afraid of the other adults at the other end of a swim, swim your child to the side, instead of to other people.

The Bottom Line

1. Bring your baby into the water from the side or step and allow the child to swim freely toward you for several seconds.
2. Encourage your child to reach for you on his or her own.
3. Teach your baby to swim to the side and hang on to the edge until you arrive.
4. Practice swimming your child to other adults and from other adults back to you.
5. To help your baby get a breath, periodically lift your child's chin above the surface.

Rolling Over

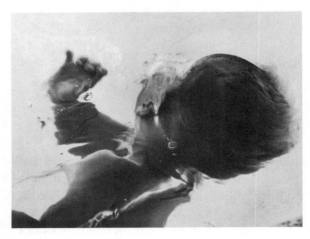

Figure 1   Rolling over to get a breath could save your baby from drowning. It is also a forerunner to learning rhythmic breathing, an important part of the front crawl stroke.

Figure 2   Lead-up exercises for rolling over can begin as soon as your baby has learned to relax in the back position. For the first lead-up exercise, rock your baby from side to side as you support the child's head.

Figure 3   In the second exercise (Figures 3, 4, 5, and 6), your baby will actually roll from the back position to the stomach position. Lay your baby's head on your shoulder, the child's feet against the wall, and move backward in the water.

Figure 4   As you move backward, count to 3. Then say "roll" and turn toward your baby, gently rolling the child onto the stomach.

Figure 5   While your baby is in the stomach position, move forward again to the count of 3.

Figure 6   Again, say ''roll'' and finish the exercise by rolling your baby back onto your shoulder. Repeat the entire rolling over process several times as you walk from one side of the pool to the other.

Figure 7 Don't switch shoulders when rolling your baby. If you do, you are forced to lift your baby awkwardly through the air.

Figure 8 Keep your baby's face out of the water during the first rolling attempts. Later, when rolling the child onto the stomach, dip the child's face underwater. Then, roll to the back position to get a breath.

Figure 9   Rolls can be practiced during swims between you and the teacher or another adult (Figures 9, 10, 11, and 12). As the teacher pushes your baby to you, use your left hand (if the baby is on your left) to grasp the child under the arm. Use your right hand to support the child's head during the roll.

Figure 10   After the roll, continue to hold your baby on his or her back, using as little support as necessary.

Figure 11   For heavier babies, the roll works better if you place your left hand (if your baby is on your left) on the child's stomach and right hand on the child's back during the roll.

Figure 12   Eventually, the roll will become automatic for your baby and you will need only one hand to start the roll. Your child will be able to complete the roll without your help.

Keys to Success

1. The primary purpose of rolling is to teach your baby how to rest and breathe in the water. Don't skip over this skill. It could save your child's life.

2. The secondary purpose of rolling over is to prepare your baby for rhythmic breathing. Although rhythmic breathing is a very efficient way of breathing when swimming, it is also very complicated and few children under age 6 master it. Compared to rhythmic breathing, rolling over is far less frustrating for young children to master, and learning it first makes learning rhythmic breathing easier when they are older.

3. Rolling over on their backs to get a breath does not mean that babies should never be taught to lift their heads when on their stomachs. However, it is easier for them to get a breath by rolling over on their backs and, thus, more likely to save their lives if they accidentally fall into the water.

4. Keep your shoulders at water level so that your baby can feel the buoyancy of the water throughout the roll.

5. Allow your baby to remain in the back position long enough to take several breaths. As your child becomes proficient in rolling, encourage your baby to roll back to the stomach after only one breath.

6. Be alert to your baby's natural way of rolling. If your baby prefers to roll to the right, roll to the right. If your child prefers to roll to the left, roll left. Once you have determined your child's preference, always roll in that direction.

7. Most babies prefer either their right or left sides, but some roll vertically, by pushing their heads back, like a backward somersault. First, they let their legs sink, and then they lay their heads back to get a breath. If your child prefers to roll

vertically, allow it. As long as it serves the purpose of allowing the child to get a breath, it is a satisfactory safety skill.

8. Be sure to use the same shoulder throughout the roll. Midroll switching is awkward. It keeps your child out of the water, rather than in it.

9. While rolling your baby between teacher and parent, use your arm if necessary to support the child's head as the roll is completed.

10. Mastery of rolling occurs when your child can roll over without any assistance, take a breath, roll back to the stomach, and continue swimming until another breath is needed.

The Bottom Line

1. Before trying an unassisted roll, practice rocking your baby from side to side in the back position—the first lead-up exercise.

2. For the second lead-up exercise, lay your baby's head on your shoulder, roll your child into the stomach position, and back onto your shoulder.

3. For a full-fledged roll, roll your baby into the back position during swims from the teacher.

4. Mastery occurs when your baby can roll to get a breath whenever one is needed.

Breath Control

Figure 1   Breath control is not only an important safety skill, but it is also a prerequisite for deep water enjoyment. There are two aspects of breath control: single breath control and intermittent breathing.

Figure 2   Bubble blowing and submersion will be your baby's first encounters with single breath control. To teach bubble blowing, put your lips in the water close to your baby's face and blow noisily to get your child's attention. It may take a while, but eventually your child will copy you.

Figure 3 Treasure diving is a more advanced version of single breath control. Before trying it, your baby should feel comfortable underwater and be capable of 5 seconds of breath holding.

Figure 4 By gradually increasing the length of swims from teacher to parent and to the side, your baby learns to take deeper breaths and hold them longer. Do not be surprised if your baby's breath-holding capacity eventually surpasses yours!

Figure 5 Dipping, chin lifting, and rolling over are all exercises that teach intermittent breathing. For dipping, hold your baby under the arms and dip the child's face in the water at regular intervals as you move backward.

Figure 6 As your baby becomes proficient at dipping, proceed to chin lifting. With your baby in the stomach position, remove your support and let the child swim toward you as you walk backwards. At regular intervals, lift the chin with your fingers so the child can get a breath. After inhalation, release your baby's chin and allow the child to swim several seconds unsupported, before you lift the chin again.

Keys to Success

1. Don't postpone breath control exercises in an attempt to protect your baby. The only way your baby can exist in the water is by learning to inhale only when the mouth or nose has access to the air. If your child never becomes proficient in breath control, swimming will be an ordeal rather than a pleasure. It is our experience that babies between 6 months and 2 years learn breath control more easily than those older. For older children, involuntary breathing without restraints has become such an ingrained habit that conscious breath control is quite difficult to teach.

2. Bubble blowing, submersion, diving, and swimming are the simplest forms of breath control. They increase your child's breath-holding capacity, as well as extend the length of time a child can hold the breath.

3. Bubble blowing is not always easy to teach to infants for two reasons. First, it is the opposite of sucking, which is one of the strongest reflexes in newborns. If your baby is less than 6 months old, your child must overcome the need to suck in and make a conscious effort to blow out. Second, most babies prefer to breathe through their noses. To blow bubbles, they must learn to use their mouths to exhale.

4. Very young babies breathe at irregular intervals, both in and out of the water, so you can't always predict your child's need for a breath. Your predictions will be more accurate, though, if you watch for the signs that indicate your child needs to breathe. These signs are scrunching up the face, exhaling bubbles, or frantic moving of the arms and legs.

5. Most babies keep their eyes open underwater in order to see where to go for safety and what to grab onto in pulling up for a breath. If your baby doesn't do this, submerge with

your child or place a toy underwater so the child has something interesting to look at while submerged. Of course, if the pool's pH factor is abnormal and the water burns your child's eyes, don't expect your baby to open its eyes no matter how interesting the underwater object is.

6. During submersions your baby learns to hold its breath while underwater, as well as to stop breathing before submersion. By increasing the amount of time you hold your baby underwater, you increase your child's breath-holding capacity.

7. Neither babies nor adults utilize the maximum capacity of their lungs, so don't worry that holding the breath for 6 or 7 seconds will harm your baby. It merely teaches your child to use more lung space.

8. If your child is asthmatic, the breath control exercises practiced in swimming can actually reduce the symptoms. Some cities have special swimming classes for asthmatics. Check with your physician, though, before beginning any swimming program.

9. Diving toys should be brightly colored and heavy enough to sink. Small rocks wrapped in red cloth work very well. Place the rock in the center of the cloth, bring the four corners together, twist, and secure with a rubber band.

10. Babies capable of standing alone have drowned in shallow water simply because they never had practice standing in water. For safety training, encourage your baby to stand up without your help after coming up from a dive. Even though the water is shallow, your baby needs to be taught how to regain footing. Otherwise, your child may fall into shallow water and flounder helplessly, never having been taught how easy it is to stand up.

11. Begin treasure diving in shallow water. Gradually increase the depth to as much as 3 feet. In deeper water, though, help your child get a breath after the dive.

12. NEVER ALLOW YOUR CHILD TO DIVE IN FROM THE SIDE IN SHALLOW WATER.

13. Dipping your child's face periodically underwater, lifting the chin at regular intervals, and rolling over give your baby practice breathing intermittently. Initially, your child may need several breaths before feeling ready to go under again. Gradually decrease the amount of time you allow for get-

ting a breath until your child can get a sufficient breath in a second or less.

14. Teach your child that it is possible to get an adequate breath even though the lips or mouth barely clear the surface. Your child will tire more quickly if the entire head is lifted out of the water every time a breath is needed. Lifting the head causes the feet to drop and actually causes the child's body and head to sink.

15. If your child is under 6 months, dipping is best done with the child held out in front of you in the stomach position. Older children can be held at your side.

16. Intermittent breathing can be mastered by children under age 3, but rhythmic breathing during the front crawl stroke is seldom mastered before age 6.

17. During the first lessons, be consistent in the amount of time you keep your baby underwater.

Eager Personality

After a few successful intermittent breathing experiences, an eager baby may think the water is totally under his or her control and may want to be under the water more than out of it. This is common in our classes and certainly one of our goals. However, your child can never be considered totally water safe and always needs to be carefully watched.

Sometimes these eager children become so excited and active in the water that they become tired without being aware of it. As their breathing becomes labored and irregular, they may misjudge when they should inhale, or the breaths they take may not be sufficiently deep. The result is a choking, disillusioned child who is reluctant to ever go under that "double-crossing" water again. To prevent this from happening to your baby, use water games as a distraction whenever your child starts getting fatigued.

Another worry we have with eager babies is premature burnout. After being underwater many times, your baby may become bored and refuse to practice underwater skills. By providing lots of varied activities, you can lessen the chance that this will happen to your child.

Cautious Personality

No matter how skilled the teacher is or how patient the parent, some babies always breathe underwater and choke. These babies, whom we call "sniffers," usually are incapable of holding their breath. If your child is a sniffer, there is little you can do but avoid underwater skills and wait until the child grows out of it. Repeated submersions will encourage your baby to hate swimming and may even cause water intoxication. If your baby is a sniffer, limit your child's submersions by dipping the child's face underwater for no more than 2 seconds. Maintain a constant rhythm for dipping and give your baby lots of cues before going underwater.

Teaching babies to keep their eyes open underwater so they can see where to swim for safety may be another problem. Most babies, after a series of lessons, will keep their eyes open on their own. Babies who refuse to open their eyes, even though the pH of the water is well-controlled, may have an allergy to the chlorine or another substance in or around the pool. If your baby develops a stuffy nose and irritated eyes shortly after entering the pool, do not insist on open eyes until you are sure an allergy is not the problem. Swimming goggles may help keep the offending substance out of your child's eyes and still allow your child to see underwater.

The Bottom Line

1. Practice the single breath control exercises of submersion, bubble blowing, diving, and swimming.
2. Later, work on the intermittent breathing exercises of dipping, chin lifting, and rolling over.
3. Gradually increase the length of underwater time.
4. Encourage your baby to keep its eyes open underwater.

7
Chapter

A Typical Lesson

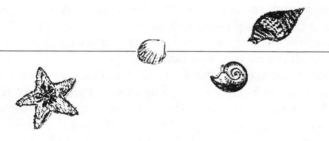

*F*ree time, skills time, and game time are the basic elements of a baby swim lesson. In this chapter, learn how to use these elements for a happy, productive lesson.

Type of Class

Just as the same size clothing does not fit everyone, the same baby class is not appropriate for all babies. Baby classes function best when all of the children are functioning at the same developmental level; the directions are more streamlined, the babies more at ease, and the parents are more comfortable interacting with other parents with whom they have a lot in common. The teachers can plan a more appropriate skill progression and choose games that reflect the entire group's developmental level. The class stays together better and moves along at a faster, more interesting pace. There are four types of classes: newborn, baby, toddler, and independent toddler.

Newborn (0 to 6 Months)

✳ Goals:

1. To facilitate water adaptation
2. To reinforce swimming reflexes
3. To encourage bonding between parent and child
4. To provide experience in the front and back position

Until 6 months of age, babies are still at the mercy of their reflexes. Few of their movements are voluntary, and most of their learning is in the form of passive listening and observation. Water adjustment is the main focus of such classes, so skills and underwater work are deemphasized.

For the first 6 weeks, most of what is done in a newborn class can be handled better in the family bathtub. During these early weeks, babies have very little motor control and tend to droop when not fully supported. They are a little easier to handle in the family tub. By the time babies are 6 weeks old, they have enough body control to be held in the front and back positions in a pool.

Newborn class

To set a quiet, soothing mood, the session usually begins with 10 minutes of infant massage and exercise on the deck area next to the pool. The exercise continues in the pool, interspersed with instructions on how to hold the babies and perform mini-dunks. Occasionally, to reinforce the swimming reflexes, the babies may be placed prone, water covering their faces, where they will kick, pull, and hold their breath. Many of the eight basic skills are practiced, but at a rudimentary level.

Lesson Recipe:
Infant Massage and Exercise—10 minutes
Water Adaptation—10 to 20 minutes

Baby (6 to 15 Months)

Goals:

1. To encourage communication between parent and child
2. To observe and socialize with other babies and adults
3. To build self-confidence
4. To practice all eight basic skills

By 6 months of age, most babies have learned to sit up and are making voluntary movements. They initiate interactions with their environment, rather than waiting passively to be entertained. Babies this age usually enjoy the new experiences they find in a watery world.

Temperamentally, babies between 6 and 15 months are easy to work with. They have not yet learned to fear the water and are eager to please. Willingly, they rely on their parents for guidance, and when it's time to go underwater they accept the consequences without blinking an eye. This dependency also makes it easier for them to lie back in the water, a position toddlers often detest.

Developmentally, they are limited in their ability to master the eight basic skills. For example, they still use a bent arm pull and kick with bent legs. They love games, even though they cannot participate directly, and are content with being carried through the actions by their parents.

To coax the babies into the routine of swimming class, it's wise to warm up with the same procedure for each lesson, preferably with a circle game. A good choice is "Ring Around the Rosies" in which the last line "we all fall down" is deleted and the words and actions "we all say hi" are substituted. The first game should be played above the water, and each successive game should be a little more adventuresome, ending with an underwater game.

The warm-up is followed by skills practice. Usually the teacher will introduce a skill first by describing it and then by demonstrating the proper technique with a cooperative baby. This is often followed by another group game that focuses on the same skill. The class then might break into individual parent-child pairs to practice, while the teacher circulates among the group offering personalized guidance for each baby. The group is brought back together where the same procedure is followed for another skill. All eight basic skills can be covered during the classtime by an advanced group, while a beginning group may cover only three.

Baby class

The last minutes of the class are spent as free time in which parent and child can do whatever they wish. When the class is finally over, getting the babies out of the pool can be a problem if you do not arrange an ending ritual. Again, "Ring Around the Rosies" is an appropriate choice because the words "we all say good-bye" can be substituted for the last line. While getting out of the pool, the babies can be distracted from their crying protests by occupying their hands and voices with waving good-bye to their friends, the teacher, the pool, and their favorite water toys.

Lesson Recipe:
Introductory Games—5 minutes
Skills Practice—20 minutes
Free Time—5 minutes
Good-bye Ritual

Toddler (15 Months to 3 Years)

Goals:

1. To develop a learning relationship based on praise
2. To master all eight basic skills with parental assistance
3. To build self-confidence
4. To provide opportunities for peer play

The biggest difference between toddler and baby classes is the fact that toddlers can walk. At home toddlers seldom get to walk enough, and the same is true at swimming class. They demand freedom to walk around and in the pool. While baby classes are spent in chest deep water to facilitate baby handling, toddlers prefer shallow water where they can practice the skills without their parents' help. Free time is extremely important to them.

Mom or Dad is still needed to remain close to their toddlers. Since 2 feet is the perfect depth for toddlers, parents have to learn "the shallow end duck walk" so they can follow their toddlers around and provide assistance. Younger toddlers may need full-time assistance, but older toddlers may prefer to be left totally alone.

Toddlers thrive on activities that allow them to be independent. Many of them can follow directions and even wait their turn. Games, especially those related to everyday routines, are their favorite part of class time, and they will repeat the songs over and over. They enjoy camaraderie with their peers during group games although they seldom seek one another out during free play.

Toddlers can do so many things—but they also reserve the right not to do them. "No" is clearly their favorite word. Temperamentally, they are more difficult than younger babies, but if they are kept happy and stimulated they are usually too busy to even think about saying "no." For this reason, fast-paced classes function best.

Lesson Recipe:
Introductory Games—5 minutes
Skills Practice—20 minutes
Free Time—5 minutes
Good-bye Ritual

Toddler class

Independent Toddler (2-1/2 to 3-1/2 Years)

Goals:

1. To provide opportunities for peer play
2. To master all eight basic skills, without parental assistance
3. To build self-confidence
4. To teach the concept of waiting for a turn

Between 2-1/2 and 3-1/2 years, toddlers are ready to graduate into a class by themselves. The precise time a toddler is ready depends on water experience, eagerness to swim underwater, age, swimming ability, and emotional level. Minor factors to consider are whether the child can follow directions, is tall enough to stand alone in the shallow end, will behave for adults other than the parents, and has at least a 1-minute attention span. Some children this age handle the separation from the parents

Independent toddler class

quite well, but others feel more secure knowing Mom or Dad is nearby. Others who have learned that having a temper tantrum will bring Mom or Dad running to rescue function better if the parents stay out of sight.

The class format is basically the same as that for toddlers, with the exception that skills time is divided into two parts: deep end and shallow end periods. During deep end practice the children cling to the side and wait their turn with the teacher, while during shallow end practice the children can stand at the side and wait their turn. In either case, the children stay together as a group and do not go off to practice by themselves until free time.

The teacher must be selective about choosing games for this group, as not all of them are adapted to a toddler without a parent.

Lesson Recipe:
Introductory Games—4 minutes
Skills Practice (Shallow End)—15 minutes
Skills Practice (Deep End)—6 minutes
Free Time—5 minutes
Good-bye Ritual

Scheduling Lessons

Thirty minutes is the maximum length of time babies are productive in the water. Extending the time is not a very efficient way of increasing learning. In fact, learning may actually decrease because as the babies tire, their performance drops, they choke more frequently, and they are more likely to become water intoxicated. Newborns last an even shorter amount of time. Depending on the water temperature, 15 minutes is about the maximum length of time newborns are productive. If the lesson ends while the babies are still happy, they will remember it in a positive light and will be eager to return.

Class Size

If you are teaching your baby on your own, you do not have to worry about the size of the class getting out of hand. However, if you are teaching your baby in a home pool, you may wish to invite another parent and baby to join you, so your baby will have a chance to develop socialization skills.

If you are enrolled in a swim school, try to find one that limits enrollment. Six babies with their parents is an ideal size for a swim class. There are just enough people to make the games fun. Much more than six and the class is transformed into an uncontrollable mob. With even seven babies, the noise level is increased enough to be nerve wracking. The babies start crying and parents, disgruntled and ignored, begin straying away from the group. If the class is composed of independent toddlers, it's essential that the group has no more than six children.

An important component of baby swim classes is the time the teacher spends alone with each parent-child pair to meet individual needs. In large classes, there is simply not enough time to make such consultations feasible. The end results are babies who are inefficiently taught and consequently do not progress. Larger classes may be cheaper, but to compensate for the lack of individualized instruction, most babies have to attend more classes to become competent.

Lesson Frequency

Babies progress faster if they have the opportunity to be in the water every day. If you have your own pool, you can usually arrange your schedule so that your baby has a daily dip in the pool. But for parents who work or who have signed up for lessons at a pool across town, such frequent classes are not feasible and may be a difficult-to-arrange luxury. Twice a week is the maximum number most parents seem to be able to manage, and though not as effective as daily scheduling, most babies do not regress excessively between classes taken twice a week. Once-a-week classes can also be effective, but only if the lessons are organized and include well-defined, limited goals. Progress will be slower, but eventually the child will master the eight basic skills.

If you and your baby are enrolled in a public swimming program, most likely you will receive eight to ten lessons. To master the eight basic skills under such an arrangement, most babies need at least three sessions (30 to 40 lessons). The more routine and repetition from session to session, the fewer adjustments babies have to make and the better their progress. Ideally, each baby would attend the same class, at the same time of day, and with the same teacher and children throughout all the sessions. Babies can tolerate up to a 6-month break between sessions without forgetting most of what they have learned. Even after such a long lapse between sessions, most babies are back in the swing of things within several lessons, especially if they have had bathtub lessons during the intersession.

A

Appendix

Health and
Safety Concerns

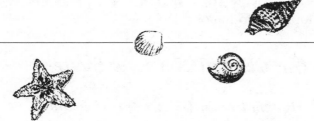

Well-maintained and monitored pools pose very little threat to you and your baby's health. Their filter systems efficiently remove unwanted solid matter while chlorine kills most germs. In fact, your home bathtub and bathwater are more likely to make you sick. Remember also that water is not the only way germs are transported. Many germs travel through the air, while others can be transmitted only through person-to-person contact. At least in pool water germs are at a disadvantage because of chlorine's killing effectiveness.

In the United States, most local public health agencies are quite zealous in enforcing their strict regulations about swimming pools. Home pools, lakes, and salt water beaches are more likely to make you sick because they aren't as well monitored or chlorinated as public pools.

Choosing a well-maintained swimming area to teach your baby to swim is extremely important to you and your baby's health. Undoubtedly, most pools are very clean, but do not make that assumption without checking it out first for yourself. Look at the surfaces around the pool. Wooden floors, cracked tile, and crumbling plaster are more likely to harbor germs than smooth, nonporous surfaces. Pool air that smells strongly of chlorine and irritates your eyes also indicates poor maintenance. Ask how often the pool is checked and adjusted for chlorine content and pH. Your local health department is also a good source of information about specific pools.

If you choose a well-cared for pool, there is no need for you to worry about swimming in "troubled" waters. There is no more risk in letting your baby play in pool water than in allowing the child to crawl across your living room carpet. The hazards that exist are relatively minor. For the few risks that do exist, it's wise to be informed so that you can spot them early and prevent them from developing into major problems.

The Central Nervous System

✳ *Hyponatremia (Water Intoxication)*

Hyponatremia, commonly called water intoxication, is a potentially fatal condition resulting from extremely high levels of water in the body.

Water intoxication can result from tap water enemas, renal disease, pulmonary disturbance, and diseases of the central nervous sytem. Recently, an increase in hyponatremia has been attributed to swallowing large amounts of water during swimming lessons. It is not known whether the actual trigger factor that causes hyponatremia is excessive sodium loss, excessive intake of free water, inappropriate secretion of antidiuretic hormone (SIADH), or a combination of all these factors.

Whatever the cause, the condition is very easy to prevent. All it takes is a little common sense. Far too often, though, parents have overlooked their common sense and have allowed their babies to be repeatedly dunked and held underwater, even when their children were obviously distressed.

Most hyponatremic babies recover with no long-term aftereffects. We do not mean to frighten you away from baby swimming classes. Most baby swim classes are not aggressively taught, nor do they hold drownproofing as their main goal. Do remember, however, that all teachers are not competent nor do they always know what is best for your baby. Carefully choose a swimming school that does not use repeated, forced dunkings as its predominant method of teaching.

A little common sense and an awareness of the symptoms of hyponatremia will help you keep your baby safe. It is not common sense to hand your baby to a stranger and stand idly by while the stranger holds your child underwater. It is not common sense to ignore your baby's terrified screams. It is not common sense to hold your baby underwater for long periods. It is smart to observe your baby's reaction and to stop the lesson as soon as you notice the child is distressed. If your baby does swallow a lot of water, becomes restless, lethargic, irritable, weak, and nauseous, and has abnormally wet diapers, the child may be suffering from hyponatremia, and you should call your doctor immediately.

Often, hyponatremia is confused with near drowning in the emergency room. Both hyponatremia and near drowning victims have been in the water, both are often wearing swimming suits, and both may have seizures and respiratory distress and fall into a coma. The wrong diagnosis can lead to delays in proper treatment, so explain to your doctor that the child has swallowed large amounts of water and may be hyponatremic. In near drownings, water usually enters the victim's lungs, whereas in hyponatremia water enters the stomach. Near drowning victims have abnormal chest radiographs, while hyponatremics do not. If water intoxication is suspected, physicians can confirm their diagnosis by analyzing arginine vasopressin levels as well as blood serum and electrolytes.

Near-drowning victims are often given anticonvulsants, which have little effect on correcting the hyponatremia. Moreover, these anticonvulsants tend to depress respiration and increase the need for assisted ventilation of the victim's lungs. The best therapy for a water intoxicated patient is the prompt administration of a saline solution, and the victim will probably recover without ever needing anticonvulsants.

Serious water intoxication is rare and should become rarer as parents learn the proper ways to submerge their babies.

1. Do not force submersion on your baby. Heed your baby's cries and protests.

2. Do not hold the child under for long periods. Three seconds is the maximum for beginning babies, and 5 seconds is the maximum for youngsters less than a year old.
3. Do not submerge the child more than three times per lesson during the initial lessons.
4. Watch your baby's face during submersion for signs that the child is swallowing large amounts of water.
5. If you suspect your baby has swallowed too much water, watch the child carefully for signs of restlessness, lethargy, irritability, nausea, and extremely wet diapers, especially if these symptoms continue for more than 4 hours after the lesson.

Ears

Fungal Infections

Fungal infections, a type of otitis externa, are confined to the outer ear canal and as such pose no serious threat to hearing. Both diseases present the same itching symptoms. Fungal infections usually develop from swimming in dirty, polluted water, especially water contaminated by sewage. In otitis externa the walls of the outer ear become red and inflamed, but in a fungal infection gray or black particles (fungi) line the canal. A physician is the only one who can make a correct diagnosis. If you believe you or your baby has such an infection, you can treat it as you would otitis externa with tufts of cotton soaked in dilute vinegar. If the itching does not go away in several days, see your physician. Hearing aid users are frequently afflicted with fungal infections as these devices tend to trap water in the ears.

Myringotomy

Traditionally, children who have a myringotomy (an incision in the eardrum to help drain fluid) and have had tubes (grommets) inserted in their ears are warned to keep water out of their ears. They are admonished not to swim and to wear a cap when bathing and showering. However, not one clinical

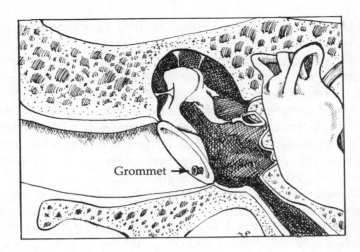

During myringotomy, also called typanotomy, a tiny incision is made in the eardrum to help drain fluid from the middle ear and to allow for a free exchange of air between the middle and outer ear.

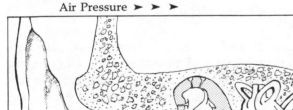

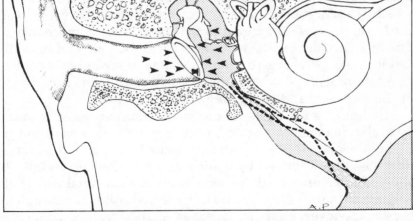

During normal swimming, excluding diving and deep underwater swims, there is seldom enough water pressure to force water through the tube.

study has had results that indicate swimming with tubes is harmful. As more and more doctors realize this and allow their patients to swim, more and more data is accumulated that proves children with grommets can swim with no adverse effects.

In a recent, very thorough study, no significant difference was found between the incidence of ear infections in swimming children with tubes and those nonswimmers with tubes (Marks, 1983). Nor was there any more middle ear drainage. Moreover, earplugs and antibacterial drops were found to be unnecessary in preventing infections after swimming.

During normal swimming, excluding diving and deep underwater swims, there is seldom enough water pressure to force water through the tube. If some water is forced through, remember it has been chlorinated and contains very few bacteria. Without a doubt, bath water is much less clean and is more likely to cause an infection. If your baby does have tubes in his ears, almost no chance exists that the child would be harmed by swimming.

Otitis Externa

Otitis externa, commonly known as swimmer's ear, is an infection of the external ear canal and a common cause of earache in children. Because the infection is confined to the outer ear, which is separated from the more delicate middle ear by the eardrum, it poses little threat to the actual hearing mechanism. The main problem with swimmer's ear is the pain and discomfort it causes. It was given the nickname of swimmer's ear because there seemed to be a relationship between the occurrence of the infection and swimming.

Swimmer's ear is one of the most common ailments faced by otolaryngologists. Usually, only one ear is involved, but in 30% of the cases it affects both ears. Initially, it is a mild bacterial infection, characterized by itching and a stuffed up feeling. If allowed to go untreated, the skin lining the ear canal will swell and secrete a sticky liquid, and the infected child may complain of pain and fever. Injury to the ear and harsh cleaning with soap and cotton swabs upset the pH balance and also predispose the ear to infection.

Swimmer's ear is not due simply to swimming or the presence of water in the ears. The actual cause of otitis externa seems to be a combination of factors. Warm air, humid air, warm water, length of time spent swimming, the natural enzymatic activity in the ear canal, and the presence of bacteria are all factors that predispose the ear to otitis externa.

As a precaution, shake your head and dry your ears and your baby's after swimming. Any ear canal that stays wet is going to become infected. Wetness may even be more important than contamination in predisposing the ear to infection. Ears that have a heavy wax accumulation can trap water inside the outer ear canal, which can also lead to otitis externa.

Some people have outer ears that are highly susceptible to otitis externa. If you or your baby repeatedly develop the disease, you may wish to purchase over-the-counter drops that dry the ear and kill bacteria. The drops contain alcohol for drying and an acidifying agent (boric acid) to inhibit bacterial and fungal growth. You can mix up a home version yourself by combining 1 pint rubbing alcohol with 3 tablespoons white vinegar (an acidifier). Using an eyedropper, place a few drops in each ear and let them remain for a minute. Let the drops drain out by tilting your head to the side.

Some people claim baby oil or olive oil is equally effective. The oil replaces wax lost by daily swimming. Others use only a drop or two of alcohol. The alcohol, which evaporates more quickly than water alone, mixes with any water left in the ear causing fast drying. Ear plugs are not effective in preventing otitis externa.

If your ears do start to itch, soak a tuft of cotton in vinegar diluted 50/50 with water and loosely insert it into the ear canal. Take a pain reliever to reduce discomfort and keep water out of the ear. Change the cotton tuft every 2 hours. If the infection does not clear up in a day or two, call your physician. Antibiotics (oral versions are not always effective in treating such ear infections) may be necessary, so see your physician.

Otitis Media

Does swimming increase your baby's chances of getting an otitis media infection, and if your baby already has otitis media, will swimming cause it to become worse? Some physicians believe there is little connection between swimming and middle ear infections, whereas others advise their patients not to swim if they are prone to the disease. This stalemate between physicians hopefully will be resolved soon, but until then you will have to decide for yourself.

Unlike an outer ear infection, uncontrolled otitis media can permanently damage your baby's hearing. The delicate middle ear is a very important part of the hearing mechanism. Located between the eardrum and the hearing nerves, a middle ear infection can cause scarring of the eardrum, which rarely results in permanent hearing damage. An infection of the middle ear can also spread to the mastoid bone and eventually damage the nerves of the inner ear. Otitis media is serious and should be closely monitored by your physician. Most cases can be controlled by antibiotics.

Children have more middle ear infections than adults. Some develop otitis media with every head cold they catch. Young people are more susceptible to such infections because their eustachian tubes are shorter and straighter than adults' and provide easy "superhighway" access for bacteria. Otitis media can come on quite suddenly, and since your baby cannot tell you he or she has an earache, the infection might go unnoticed until your baby cries from the pain. Common symptoms of otitis media include fever, irritability, ear discharge, and a baby who pulls at the ears. Obviously, any baby who is not feeling well should be allowed to recuperate before being taken swimming.

Congestion, whether viral, anatomic, or allergic, provides the right conditions for bacteria to multiply and is thus the primary cause of otitis media. Bacteria also play an important role, but unless the eardrum is broken, bacteria cannot enter the middle ear via water present in the outer ear.

Eyes

Burning Sensation

Although your eyes may burn and feel irritated in the swimming pool and several hours after going home, the chlorine is so highly diluted that its effects are minor and cause no serious harm to the eyes. Actually, the chlorine dissolved in the water has very little to do with making your eyes burn. That unpleasant symptom is more the result of water that has a slightly acidic pH, a condition that is easily corrected by adding alkaline stabilizers to the water.

Contagious Conjunctivitis

Pink eye, the most common form of conjunctivitis, is highly contagious and can be transmitted through the water as well as by the air and person-to-person contact. It's highly unlikely that you or your baby would acquire pink eye from swimming. The organism causing the disease is very sensitive to low levels of chlorine. Properly maintained pools have more than enough chlorine to kill the germ. To catch pink eye you generally must have close physical contact with an afflicted person.

Hazy Vision

Hazy vision is a benign condition that often affects persons who swim for long periods in fresh water. This haziness is frequently accompanied by the phenomenon of seeing rainbows and halos around lights, sensitivity to light, and slight discomfort and tearing. The condition poses no long-term threat to your eyes and usually disappears within 30 minutes.

For most people, the hazy vision presents no significant problem, but if it bothers you, some swelling can be prevented by closing your eyes occasionally during long swims or by wearing goggles. If the hazy vision remains more than 30 minutes after the lesson and if it's accompanied by pain and redness, see your doctor.

Goggles

If wearing goggles relieves your discomfort, do not wear them so often you end up with raccoon eyes. The effect is not harmful, but it can cause discoloration around the eyes wherever the neoprene rubber of the goggles touches the skin.

Most goggle designs are inappropriate for children. There have been quite a few incidents of permanent eye injury in children that were directly caused by goggles. Usually the children were pulling the goggles away from their faces to see better or clear them of fog. The goggles slipped out of their wet fingers and sprang back, hitting their eyes with enough force to scratch them.

It would be safer to use a less elastic strap for children or even a nonelastic adjustable strap. Babies usually find goggles a nuisance anyway and will only leave them on for several seconds. In most instances it is not worth your time to purchase goggles for your baby.

The Gastrointestinal System

Enteroviruses

Enteroviruses is a generic term that includes most viruses that attack the stomach and intestines. Associated symptoms include diarrhea, rash, and vomiting. Most such illnesses are mild and easily fought off by the body's own defense system, which is fortunate because medicinal cures for enteroviruses are rare. Chlorine at recommended levels is a very effective killer of enteroviruses, and in a properly maintained pool you have little chance of catching one. On the other hand, swimming in lakes, especially polluted ones, carries a much greater risk of contracting an enterovirus.

Giardiasis Lambliasis

Giardia, as it is commonly known, has recently made newspaper headlines in the mountains where backpackers in remote areas contract the disease by drinking the water in streams and lakes. It is a highly contagious disease, characterized by diarrhea and severe intestinal cramps. It is spread through drinking water contaminated with the feces of afflicted animals and people. There is some indication that chlorine kills most of the organisms, but some strains are resistant to the normal levels of chlorine found in public pools. If you suspect you or your baby have giardia, skip your swimming lesson and see a physician lest you start an epidemic.

Handicapped

Swimming is the perfect exercise for babies with musculoskeletal diseases. The biggest obstacle these special babies face on land is gravity. Babies suffering from muscular dystrophy, spina bifida, and cerebral palsy can maneuver their bodies much more easily in the water.

In the water, they are weightless and can do things that are impossible for them to do on land. If your baby is handicapped, try to find a swimming class taught by a swimming teacher trained in adaptive aquatics. If no such class is available, your baby can still profit from learning how to swim in a regular baby class.

The Musculoskeletal System

Nursemaid's elbow is a common injury of babies who are repeatedly pulled to stand by one arm or pulled through the water too energetically by one arm. Be gentle. Your baby's joints are fragile. The cartilage in your baby's joints is less resistant to stress than cartilage in an adult. Overuse or overrotation of the joints can cause permanent damage. The rolling over maneuver and pulling, if performed improperly, can gradually weaken cartilage in the shoulder. When rolling your baby over, use the upper arm to gently turn the child onto the back. Do not jerk or put stress on the shoulder joint. The same holds true for pulling. When manipulating your baby's arms for pulling, use short motions that do not involve the shoulder.

Forcing the child's arms into unnatural positions can also create muscle imbalance. Most babies naturally keep their elbows bent, so do not attempt to force them straight in order to teach them to pull more powerfully. For the first 3 years of your baby's life, the pulling motion of the arms should resemble that of the dog paddle. Later, your child will be ready to straighten the arms during swimming.

Nose

Occasionally, your baby will sniff water up his or her nose. This hurts and your baby will probably cry and scrunch up his or her face while trying to remove the water. Beyond the discomfort, however, the chlorinated water will not cause any permanent damage. The best thing to do is console your child and forget the incident.

If your baby has a bad head cold, it's best to keep the child above the water. Because the child has difficulty breathing through the nose, a baby is more likely to keep the mouth open and swallow large amounts of water when submerged, possibly leading to water intoxication. Mild colds, however, pose few problems. In fact, the warm, moist pool air actually helps to clear the sinuses and makes breathing easier.

Skin

Feet

Athlete's foot and plantar warts are the two most common skin infections associated with swimming. The risk of infection lies not so much in the water as on the surfaces surrounding the pool. If the floors are properly disinfected and made of a non-porous product, there is little chance of developing an infection. Both the fungi causing athlete's foot and the virus causing warts are killed by chlorine. Keeping your feet clean and dry and wearing cotton socks or sandals after swimming help prevent infection.

Rash

Swimming may be relaxing, but it does have its drawbacks—you may develop a skin rash. Likewise, swimming in a bromated pool also increases your chances of breaking out into a rash. Usually the rash is totally benign and is merely the result of dry skin.

Several factors contribute to this dryness. One, the chemicals used in the water wash away the skin's natural oils that protect the skin both from dryness and infection. Two, the alternating wet and dry cycles as you get in and out of the water cause much of the skin's natural moisture to evaporate. Three, the sun dries out the skin making it feel tight and itchy. Newborns, especially, are very susceptible to the sun's drying and damaging effects and should be kept out of direct sunlight until they are at least 2 months of age. Four, the alkalinity of the water strips the skin of its natural pH and leaves it unprotected against infection. While pool water is slightly alkaline, skin is mildly acidic. This acidity kills many germs before they can penetrate the skin. Some dermatologists believe that replacing the skin's acidity by applying a pH balanced moisturizer protects your skin from not only dryness and itchiness, but also from infection.

In recent years, especially in hot tubs, the *pseudomonas aeruginosa* organism has caused several skin rash epidemics. Certain strains of the organism seem to be resistant to recommended chlorine concentrations. They especially thrive in the warm water commonly found in hot tubs. In addition to rash, the organism may cause ear infections, fever, lethargy, and painful breasts. The rash generally appears on the trunk, chest, and pelvis a few days (8 to 48 hours) after exposure. It is less commonly found on the limbs, head, and neck. Generally, the symptoms disappear on their own and a doctor is not needed.

While it is true that the strain is more resistant to chlorine than other organisms, with a little extra effort it can be killed. If *pseudomonas aeruginosa* is suspected to be causing an outbreak of rashes, the pool should be carefully monitored at least every 2 hours, and the pH level should be kept between 7.4 and 7.6. The chlorine level should be maintained at 2.0 ppm. Wooden surfaces around the pool should be superchlorinated.

Ringworm

Ringworm is rare, but it can be a problem if parts of the skin are kept continually moist. There have been several recent incidences of ringworm in children wearing polyurethane casts who disregarded their doctor's instructions on care of the cast. If you or your baby wears such a cast, drying it thoroughly after swimming and keeping it clean will prevent ringworm. If ringworm does develop, it is easily cared for by antifungal therapy. See your physician.

Temperature

For the first several weeks of life, your newborn cannot tolerate great swings in temperature, hot or cold. When the air or water surrounding a newborn cools slightly, the baby is less able to compensate for the change than an adult. Like an adult, your baby can constrict the blood vessels in the skin and conserve some body heat, but the child probably is unable to shiver in order to increase metabolism and body heat. Hypothermia can set in very quickly in babies.

Neither can your baby tolerate extreme heat. Even though the child can dilate the blood vessels and release some sweat to reduce the body's temperature, the amount of sweat produced is too small for efficient cooling. To keep your baby happy and healthy when swimming, stay out of drafts and swim in warm, not hot, water.

Yeast Infections

Swimming in chlorinated pools can increase a woman's chances of getting vaginal infections. Some physicians also believe that the chlorine kills off the normal protective bacteria, allowing abnormal yeast fungi to flourish. Women wearing tampons are especially vulnerable. The result is a yeast or vaginal infection characterized by itching and a thick, white vaginal discharge. If you spend a lot of time in the water, change from your swimming suit to a loose fitting cotton garment as soon as possible. Chlorine can interact with certain materials in bathing suits and irritate the vulva. Suits made of manmade fibers do not breathe as well as cotton and keep the vaginal area warm and moist—an ideal environment for infection.

✳ Drowning Prevention

If a child is going to die under age 4 in an accident, odds are 1 out of 7 that accident will be a drowning. Drowning is the second greatest accidental cause of death in children after motor vehicle accidents. In water-oriented areas like Arizona, California, and Florida, that death rate rises to 1 out of 3. In most cases the hapless children were merely playing adjacent to a body of water before the accident occurred. Many were playing with flotation toys, especially inner tubes and inflatable rafts.

Usually the death happened near home and not at a public pool or beach. Unsupervised swimming areas, such as backyard, hotel, and motel pools claimed the lives of many young victims. Often the pool was shallow as in fish ponds or decorative pools. Frequently, the death pool came in the guise of a bathtub. In 1976, 64 children younger than age 5 drowned in bathtubs, 24 of which were infants less than a year old.

Three fourths of all drowning victims are male. In 1-year-old children, twice as many boys as girls drown. Two-year-olds are the most likely age group to die in the water. Most victims are found fully clothed.

Typically, the accident occurs around 4:00 p.m. on a weekend or a Monday in a home with a backyard pool. Mom, busy with household chores, periodically checks on her 2-year-old. Assured that her child is playing in the house or at least away from the pool, she allows herself to be distracted by the phone or gets caught up in dinner preparation. Fifteen minutes later she checks on her child again only to discover that the child is missing. Horrified, she frantically searches everywhere, saving the pool for last because she is so sure that her child did not go near the pool. Thirty minutes later her baby's fully clothed body is dragged from the water, and the child is pronounced dead at the scene.

Given the right set of conditions, anyone can drown, including Olympic swimmers, lifeguards, and drownproofed babies. Swimming lessons may prevent some drownings, but as a baby's confidence in his or her abilities increases, there is an increased likelihood that the child will enjoy playing in the water and will venture too close when no one is looking.

Far more important than swimming lessons in drowning prevention is water safety training. Teach your baby how to stand up in the shallow end, swim to the side, or turn around and grab the side if a fall into the water occurs. More advanced water safety skills include teaching your toddler to roll or lift the head to get a breath. Especially impress on your baby never to play near the water unless you are watching.

Far more important than swimming lessons in drowning prevention is water safety training. Teach your baby how to stand up in the shallow end, swim to the side, or turn around and grab the side if she should fall in.

Training yourself to be safety conscious is even more likely to prevent your baby's drowning than any training you give your child. Constantly supervise your baby when near the water, no matter how well the child swims, even if lifeguards are present. It's impossible for even the most watchful lifeguard to keep track of everyone.

If there are any backyard pools in your neighborhood, make sure they are adequately fenced. The fence should enclose the pool entirely, with spaces between the fenceposts no more than 3 inches wide so your child cannot slip through. The holes in the fence must be too small for toddler-sized feet to gain a toe-hold and too high to climb. Pool gates should be equipped with self-closing, self-locking mechanisms. If the pool is your own, be as consistent about locking the gate as you are about zipping your pants.

If you own a backyard pool, consider purchasing a pool alarm that warns you whenever someone falls in the pool. Closed circuit TV is a more expensive way of supervising the pool, but it is useful only as long as someone monitors the screen. Pool covers, if they are the type that extend completely over the top of the pool and are guaranteed to support a child's weight, can also prevent drowning. Other kinds can actually cause drowning by inviting the child to test out the surface of the pool cover by walking on it, and the child is dropped underneath the water and becomes entrapped under the cover.

Make sure that the water level is just below the pool's rim so your child can reach the top edge and escape in an emergency.

If you own your own pool, a wise investment of time would be a water safety course in which you would learn how to administer mouth-to-mouth resuscitation and how to carry a child while swimming.

* First Aid for Drowning

Never assume a motionless, drowning baby is dead. The life preserving effects of the diving response (cessation of breathing, low body temperature, pupil dilation, cyanotic blue skin, and a slow heart beat) make victims appear dead, even when they are not. Sometimes the heart is beating so weakly even trained paramedics cannot detect a pulse. Even the duration of submersion can fool you. Although the longer the baby is underwater the less likely is survival, submerged victims have recovered after spending over 30 minutes underwater. Proceed on the assumption that prompt, prolonged resuscitation will revive the child. Do not declare the youngster dead. That decision belongs to hospital personnel.

Nor should you assume that a child who quickly recovers and whose heart and breathing are normal is out of danger. Many recovered victims survive the drowning only to die several days later from shock lung, cardiac arrest, chemical pneumonia (from aspiration of gastric contents), and pulmonary edema. Termed secondary, late, delayed, or parking lot drownings, the victims are sent home as soon as they regain consciousness and never receive needed follow-up treatment.

If you happen to be first on the scene when a drowning baby is pulled out of the water, call for someone to summon a rescue unit immediately, no matter how dead or alive the child appears. If you have had a first aid course, you will know how to administer mouth-to-mouth resuscitation and CPR.

Hypothermic Drowning

Cold water victims with hypothermia require additional first aid. Once again the decision is not easy; hypothermic babies cannot tell you their condition. Cold water is a relative term and what is cold to one person is warm to another. Cold water currents frequently pass through warm lakes, and even in heated pools the temperature is cooler near the bottom.

If hypothermia is suspected, remove the child's wet clothing and shelter the child from cold wind. Gradually start rewarming the youngster, preferably by skin-to-skin contact and wrapping the victim in blankets. Too fast rewarming can cause immediate death by sending cold blood from the arms and legs directly into the heart, causing arrythmia, which can result in a heart attack.

Continue first aid efforts even if there is no heartbeat. In many cases an obvious heartbeat does not reoccur until the child has begun to rewarm. Do not give up until the victim regains normal body temperature and still shows no vital signs. Usually we think of death and cold bodies as going together, but in the case of hypothermia the watchwords should be warm and dead. As with any drowning, the decision that a child is dead belongs to hospital personnel.

Common Hazards

Diving Boards

The depth of the pool should be at least 9-1/2 feet, while the width of the pool in the diving area should be at least 20 feet. Only one person is permitted on the diving board at any single time. Divers should check before diving to make sure the water is deep enough and no one is in the way. Children should be told to jump only once, otherwise they can slip and fall, grazing their bodies against the board on their way down. Flips and fancy dives should be done only by competent swimmers, not precocious toddlers. Diving or jumping off the board should be delayed until children are at least 2-1/2 years old. The pressure on the body caused by jumping from a height can force water into the anus, vagina, eyes, ears, and nose.

Slides

Use adult slides only if someone is in the pool to catch the child. An adult also should place the child on the slide and slide the child slowly down from a position no more than halfway up the slide, maintaining contact with the child's body until he or she drops off the end.

Decks

Numerous children are injured every year from running and accidentally falling on the pool deck or into the water. Teach your child to walk around the pool.

Shallow Water

Year after year children become paraplegics by diving into the shallow end of the pool. Adults, too, sweaty from a hot day, eagerly race toward the cool water and dive into its sometimes shallow depths. The price paid for running and leaping before looking is a broken neck and a life sentence to a wheelchair.

Lightning

Whenever lightning is 10 seconds or less away (count the number of seconds between the lightning and the later sound of thunder), all swimmers should leave the water and take shelter in a low building.

B
Appendix

Toys and Games

You and your baby's enjoyment of water can be enhanced through the use of toys and games. However, your baby will not learn to swim sooner by using swimming aids or toys. If used too much, they can become crutches that actually prevent your baby from learning to swim. Reserve their use primarily for free time. Following are some suggestions and cautions for choosing toys. A separate section provides a variety of games.

Toys

Scrounge around in your child's toy chest for favorite toys. Simple, floating toys brought from home can help your child relax and enjoy the lessons. Balls, especially ping-pong and nerf balls, are great water toys because they float and are easily grasped by tiny hands. Don't use balls so small that your baby could choke on them!

Hula hoops are very versatile water toys and can be used to encourage underwater swimming. Weighted ones work best. Your baby may enjoy swimming through the hoop underwater or jumping into it from the side.

Arm floats are commonly seen in classes for young children, but before insisting that your baby wear them, consider their usefulness for your particular case. Your baby may not need them, and may even consider them to be a nuisance.

There are three types of arm floats. Type A is inflated all around, making it unstable and thus unsuitable for babies. Type B is inflated over the top of the arm and has a flat band that wraps under the arm. Type C is composed of three sections, each separately inflatable. Although arm floats support babies' arms above the water, their heads may dip beneath the surface. They also promote a poor swimming position.

Styrofoam cubes, like arm floats, will hold your baby higher in the water and enable the child to kick and pull around the pool alone. Unfortunately, they promote a worse swimming position than do arm floats while being less versatile, as they can't be used on the back.

Inner tube-type accessories are practically useless in teaching swimming and were not designed to function as life preservers. They have also been implicated in the drownings of many children. You would be wise to restrict their use to well supervised play time after the lesson. Inner tube-type toys cause children to drown in three main ways. One, children fall out of them, and their frantic, flailing around to regain their hold only pushes the devices farther away. Two, children can propel themselves into deeper water, unaware there is a tiny leak in their float. Parents may not notice their children slowly sinking out of sight until it's too late. Third, children wearing such devices who roll over onto their backs or sides or somehow get their faces down in the water often find the floats prevent them from lifting their heads to get a breath.

Kickboards help develop kicking and strengthen the leg muscles of babies older than 8 months. To use, hold your child's hands or arms on the kickboard and tow your baby around the pool saying "kick, kick, kick." Make sure your youngster's chest rests on the kickboard itself, otherwise your child will have difficulty seeing where he or she is going.

Like kickboards, empty plastic bottles (rinsed and with the lid securely attached) also help develop arm and leg strength. Although very young babies can't use them, older babies can hold onto their handles and kick around the pool. Choose a bottle small enough for your baby to grasp easily. The main disadvantage of plastic bottles is their instability, which can cause babies to lose their balance and roll under the water. Filling the containers with a little water stabilizes them.

Small, colorful, sinking objects, such as rubber rings or rocks wrapped in red cloth, are great for older babies learning to swim underwater or for babies having difficulty opening their eyes underwater. First, show the object to your baby who is standing or being held in waist-deep water. Then, tell the child to retrieve it. For initial dives, toss it into the water no deeper than half your child's height. Never allow your child to dive after the object from a height such as the side of the pool. As your child masters diving and retrieval in shallow water, you can gradually progress to deeper water. If your baby tends to float back to the surface before retrieving the toy, try again only this time gently push your child's head toward the bottom.

A portable, plastic slide placed in shallow water is a fun way to practice submersion. Set your baby at the top of the slide and lightly pull the child underwater. Watch carefully for signs your baby has closed up before submerging! Toddlers enjoy climbing up and sliding down by themselves.

Water jungle gyms or bridges are also versatile swimming aids. When set in the middle of the pool, your baby may enjoy swimming to the bridge, pulling up to stand, and being independent a few moments before swimming back to you. It also makes a great resting spot for toddlers who can't swim all the way across the pool.

While toys can contribute to your child's learning enjoyment, be aware that overuse can lead to abuse. Oodles of toys and swimming aids crowding the pool cause confusion and interfere with learning to swim. For each lesson, it's best to limit the number of swimming aids to prevent distracting clutter.

Be especially careful about overusing floating toys with babies who have no fear of the water. Such children confidently paddle away from their parents while being supported by swimming floats, but for their own safety, they must learn the dangers of water. Parents of this type of child must supervise them carefully and should give them many opportunities, unhindered by floating devices, to discover the real nature of the water.

Swimming aids may be most useful for babies who are apprehensive about swimming. Toys and games can distract them from their worry. However, the cautiousness that leads them to worry about the water may also lead to reluctance to play with unfamiliar toys. They may respond best to favorite toys brought from home. If a new swimming aid is used, it should be introduced slowly and without force.

Games

A complete list of games that can be played while swimming would be endless. Included here are those games that we have found to be age transcendent, skill oriented, and easily learned. We encourage you to both sample these games and to invent your own to complement the skills your baby is practicing. The games can be used in class or group settings as well as by an individual parent teaching a child.

Ring Around the Rosies

> *Ring around the rosies,*
> *Pocket full of posies.*
> *Ashes, ashes,*
> *We all fall down.*

Procedure: Holding their babies, parents move in a circle. When the words "we all fall down" are sung, everyone goes underwater.

Purposes:

1. When done at the beginning of every class, it becomes part of the routine and signals the start of the lesson.
2. It reinforces commonly used actions, such as forming a circle.
3. Parents can practice holding their babies in the front and back positions.

Variations:

1. For the last line in the song different swimming skills can be substituted. For example, "we all blow bubbles," "we all wave hi," or "we all wave bye."

Ring Around the Rosies

2. For beginning babies, going under should not be done the first lesson. Instead, other actions, such as going up or going around should be substituted.
3. Toddlers can play the game in shallow water without adult help.

Motor Boat

Motor boat, motor boat go so slow.
Motor boat, motor boat go so fast.
Motor boat, motor boat step on the gas.

Procedure: Parents, holding their babies in the front or back positions, move in a circle. While singing "go so slow," the action moves slowly. For "go so fast," the action is more speeding. At "step on the gas," parents whirl their babies around in a circle on the surface of the water.

Purposes:

1. The increase in speed helps babies become more adventuresome and confident in the water.
2. It provides parents with practice holding their babies in the front and back position.

Motor Boat

Big Circle, Little Circle

Procedure: Parents form a small circle while holding their babies in the back position. All the babies' feet are touching in the center of the circle. While the teacher counts to 5 the children lie quietly with their legs down. At the count of 5, everyone says "kick, kick, kick" and while the babies kick, the parents move backward forming a large circle. The babies are then rolled to their stomachs and told to kick and pull while being directed back toward the center of the circle.

Purposes:

1. Because the children must listen for the count of 5 before kicking, they learn to wait patiently and listen for the proper cue.

2. It provides practice in the front and back position while kicking and pulling.
3. While the children's toes are together, the teacher can place his or her hands on the babies' feet to keep the legs down, helping them maintain the proper body position.

Big Circle, Little Circle

Pushing Against the Wall

Procedure: While on their backs, with heads on their parent's shoulders, the babies push their feet against the wall on the counts of 1 and 2. On 3 they push hard enough to propel themselves away from the wall. They are told to "kick, kick, kick" as their parents move backwards. As they near the other side of the pool, they are rolled to their stomachs and encouraged to grab the edge.

Purposes:

1. Babies practice kicking while on their backs.
2. As they near the far side of the pool, the babies learn to grab the edge for safety.
3. The babies gain extra experience in rolling.

Variations:

1. When the far side is reached, the babies can be pushed toward the wall and told to swim to the wall and climb out on their own.
2. By rolling repeatedly during the journey across the pool, the emphasis on the lesson can be changed from kicking to rolling.
3. After pushing a few feet away from the wall, the babies can be returned to the same wall with feet first. This allows them to watch where they are going while on their backs.

Pushing Against the Wall

Taking a Nap

Procedure: Toddlers take turns with the teacher who supports them in the back position while counting to 5. On "5," the teacher pretends to wake them up by making a ringing alarm clock sound and lifting the child to an upright position.

Purposes:

1. This game allows toddlers to act out everyday activities and practice the back position.
2. The children tend to relax more in the back position as they pretend to shut their eyes and go to sleep. Successful independent back floating is highly dependent on the ability to relax while lying back.
3. Those babies reluctant to lie back will often submit to this game, knowing that they only have to lie back for a limited, predictable amount of time (5 seconds).

Variations:

1. Advanced toddlers can count to 5 with the teacher and make a ringing alarm sound to wake up their classmates.
2. The children can pretend to eat lunch, drink some milk, or drive a car before taking a nap.

Taking a Nap

Hands Up, Hands Down

*Hands up, hands down, splash, splash, splash
Hands up, hands down, splash, splash, splash
Hands out, hands in, hands out, hands in,
Splash, splash, splash
Push down in the water, push down in the water,
Splash, splash, splash
Pull, and pull, and pull
Frog pull, frog pull, frog pull.*

Procedure: While facing the teacher with babies in their laps, parents move to the teacher's directions. Parents should sit chest high in the water on an underwater bench or lean against the side of the pool making a seat with their leg.

Hands Up, Hands Down

Purposes:

1. Because the directions vary from lesson to lesson, the babies learn to listen and follow directions.
2. The different exercises strengthen the babies' arms and provide pulling practice.

Variations:

1. Older babies should be encouraged to follow the teacher's directions without parental assistance.
2. Pulling can be in the form of an alternate arm pull or a simultaneous pull.

Humpty Dumpty

Humpty Dumpty sat on a wall
Humpty Dumpty had a great fall.

Procedure: While singing the song, the babies sit on the edge close together, swaying from side to side. On the word "fall," parents bring their children into the water.

Purposes:

1. Because the cues leading up to the fall are so pronounced, babies are more likely to close, making their submersions more successful and fun.
2. The game can be changed to accommodate swimming, breath-holding, pulling, kicking, rolling, diving, climbing to the side, and climbing out of the water after the "fall."

Variations:

1. Beginning babies can be held above the surface rather than submerged after being brought in the water after the "fall."
2. For advanced babies, parents should step back a few feet and encourage their babies to kick and pull to them after the "fall."

3. Before beginning the game, babies can hold onto the side of the pool and climb out and sit down all by themselves, a good safety skill. Turning around and grabbing the side is also a good safety skill.
4. Babies can place their hands on their heads and be brought in the water head first, to practice diving.
5. Some babies need no parental assistance at all. When the teacher gives permission, they can climb out, sit down, fall in, and swim to their parents.

Humpty Dumpty

Jack Be Nimble

Jack be nimble
Jack be quick
Jack jump over
The candlestick.

Procedure: As the babies stand on the edge of the pool, their parents help them jump into the water on the word "jump." This exercise is unsuitable for babies who are unable to stand alone.

Jack Be Nimble

Purposes:

1. The children learn not to be afraid of entering the water from a height of one to two feet.
2. Jumping in the water helps develop differentiated movement in the knees and ankles as opposed to using the leg as one whole unit. This ability usually doesn't develop until after age 2.
3. Once in the water the babies learn to hold their breath until their parents retrieve them.

Variation:

For additional practice swimming and turning around to grab the side, the parents can instruct the children to get out of the water on their own after jumping in.

Mulberry Bush

Here we go round the Mulberry Bush
The Mulberry Bush, the Mulberry Bush.
Here we go round the Mulberry Bush
So early in the morning.

Procedure: While the babies are held in the side position on their stomachs, their parents move in a circle. On the word "morning," the babies are rolled onto their backs with their heads resting on their parent's shoulders. The song is sung again, but this time the babies are rolled back onto their stomachs.

Purpose:

The babies practice rolling.

Mulberry Bush

Variation:

Using the same melody, the following lyrics may be substituted.

> *This is the way we pull our arms*
> *Pull our arms, pull our arms*
> *This is the way we pull our arms,*
> *So early in the morning.*

> *This is the way we float on our backs*
> *Float on our backs, float on our backs,*
> *This is the way we float on our backs,*
> *So early in the morning.*

Pancakes

> *I'm a little pancake on my back.*
> *I'm a little pancake nice and flat.*
> *I'm a little pancake on my back.*
> *Flip me over just like that.*

Procedure: Parents move in a circle while holding their babies on their backs with the babies' heads on their parents' shoulders. On the word "flat," parents pat the babies' stomachs. On the word "flip," the babies are rolled over onto their stomachs.

Purposes:

1. The babies practice rolling.
2. The babies practice lying quietly in the back position.

Variation:

Advanced babies can be rolled underwater and moved forward a few seconds before being brought to the surface.

Pancakes

Appendix

Tubtime

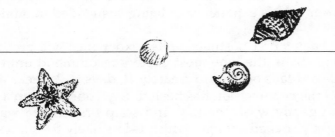

A well-planned bath is like your favorite movie—an experience you'll want to repeat. If you have 30 minutes to spare and your baby is rested and not hungry, add a special touch to the day by giving your baby a bath. Take your time, talk with your baby, and pay close attention to your child's responses. You both will emerge renewed and relaxed.

Make Bathtime Special

Think of bathtime as an unhurried, relaxed oasis. When you get in the tub with your baby, the warm water and quiet room will envelop you in a pleasurable bonding experience. Shut the door, turn off the television, and leave the phone off the hook. With the outside world at bay, you and your baby can tune into each other with all of your senses.

Clear your mind of misconceptions about baby's bath. Though you may believe that it's the time to meticulously clean your child, it's not. Babies simply don't get that dirty; all they need is a mild rinsing with soap and water.

Neither should you perceive bathtime as dangerous and frightening. Babies do not have an inborn fear of water, nor will they develop one if the bath is handled correctly. Your baby's bath is a special opportunity to relax while getting your baby a bit cleaner and teaching the child basic swimming techniques and positive attitudes toward water.

Start Soon After Birth

Some people believe that early submersion in water capitalizes on your baby's experience of being suspended in liquid *in utero*.

Your baby's first postnatal water experience will probably be a sponge bath, the type most doctors recommend until the umbilical cord falls off (approximately 10 days to 2 weeks after birth) and the circumcision has healed. Lay your child on a dry towel and gently wash the face and scalp first. Use a warm, damp, lightly soaped sponge, which is less likely than a washcloth to release those irritating drips that are so unnerving to your baby. Rinse with a warm, damp sponge. Repeat the same procedure for the rest of the body, saving the baby's bottom until last to reduce contamination on the sponge. Pay special attention to cleaning skin folds and creases where dirt and bacteria have a tendency to collect.

Get in With Your Baby

If you have a newborn, ignore those tempting ads for special baby tubs and devices. For newborns, the family bathtub works much better because you can get in with your baby. That way you can give as much support and physical closeness as your baby needs. Quite the contrary happens with special baby tubs, which force you to hold your baby away from your body, making both you and the child feel uneasy.

Baths in the family tub also establish an early awareness and acceptance of the water. Baths will probably be your baby's first conscious experience in water since newborn swimming classes are rare and many physicians do not recommend pool swimming until babies are at least 3 months old.

Set the "Stage"

Before hopping in the tub, gather all needed bathing supplies within an arm's reach of the tub. There are lots of specialized baby bath supplies, but only four items are truly needed: tearless baby shampoo, a sponge, a towel, and lotion or oil in a plastic container. Prewarm the cream or oil by soaking it in the tub while you bathe your baby. Most brands of baby products are reliable, but be cautious when choosing a shampoo. Some brands claim to be tearless, but they still burn enough to make your baby cry. If switching brands doesn't help, use a very dilute amount of shampoo.

Keep Your Baby Warm

The water should be deep enough to cover at least half of your baby's body when the child is in a supine position—approximately 2 inches in a portable baby tub and 6 inches in the family bathtub. Deeper water also allows you to reduce the air temperature in the bathing area. If your baby is in shallow water or is held up out of the water by a sponge or other aid, the air temperature should be at least 75° F (24° C). When submerged, your baby will be kept warm by the water and not the air. This allows you to bathe your baby in rooms with air temperatures as low as 68° F (20° C). Just remember to wrap your infant in a towel as soon as you lift her out of the water.

Water temperature should be between 90° F (32° C) and 95° F (35° C). Always test it with your wrist or elbow before getting in the tub. The water should feel neither hot nor cold. A thermometer is not necessary. Even if you have one, recheck the temperature with your wrist or elbow. Bath water thermometers are notorious for malfunctioning.

Use a Comfortable, Secure Position

The following unfortunate scenario is far too common. Mom or Dad, believing that the bathtub water is scary and harmful, try to hold their child out of the water throughout the bath. However, holding a soapy, slippery baby out of the water is an awkward, frustrating task. Both baby and parent are uncomfortable and sense that their position is precarious. As worry and tension mount, they both break down in tears, convinced that bathtime is a horrible experience.

Bathtime should be a happy experience. First, you must realize that laying your baby back in the water is not harmful. Actually, the soothing, warm water relaxes your baby, enabling you to carry out the cleaning process effortlessly and without having to wrestle a protesting, squirming baby. Rather than your wet, slippery hands supporting most of your baby's weight, the tub or your legs do the supporting, freeing your hands for washing and holding your child's arms to prevent a Moro reflex. Occasionally, you may need to stabilize your baby's head with your hand to prevent it from rolling to the side and under the water's surface. (Be careful not to touch the child's cheeks or you'll set off the rooting reflex.) Usually, though, your baby will look straight up at you and not roll to the side.

While lying back, your baby will experience the sensation of water in the ears and will gradually become accustomed to

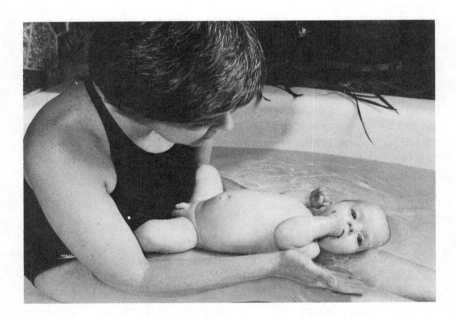

While lying back, your baby will experience the sensation of water in his ears, and gradually will become accustomed to the feeling.

the feeling. It's best if the water level is past your baby's ears and does not fluctuate above and below them, since this is distracting to the child. Later, in swimming lessons, those early experiences with water in the ears will help the child accept the back floating position.

If you are using a portable, plastic baby tub, you may wish to lay a towel in the bottom to make a softer bed for your baby, but the towel will bunch up in the water and is probably more trouble than it's worth. Most babies do not even notice the firm bottom anyway. But, if you're determined to soften the bottom, you may wish to purchase a large, flat, baby bath sponge for your child to lie on.

Be Assured the Water Won't Damage Your Baby's Ears

Unless your baby has a perforated eardrum, it's impossible for water in the outer ear canal to flow into the middle or inner ear where ear infections start. Remind yourself that throughout pregnancy your baby's ears were harmlessly filled with fetal fluid. Nine months in water didn't cause ear damage and neither will 15 minutes in the tub.

Use Soap Sparingly

Most hard to wash spots are not dirty enough to warrant poking around with finger tips or cotton swabs to get them clean. Such poking usually will only make your baby cry. Except for unusual circumstances, a soft washcloth or sponge does a sufficient job. Shampoo and soap should be used sparingly. Some doctors recommend that you avoid soap altogether and use clear water only.

Shampoo Fearlessly

Shampooing too gently is far more common than shampooing too vigorously. Your baby's scalp is quite tough and needs a thorough scrubbing. To avoid cradle cap, a common disorder appearing as dirty, waxy patches on the scalp, massage a tear-free shampoo into the scalp with your fingertips (not fingernails). Rinse thoroughly. Use only small amounts of water and shampoo as too much liquid only ends up running down your child's face. If cradle cap persists or if your baby's scalp becomes red or encrusted, consult your doctor.

Dry Off Quickly

Even on warm days the evaporation of water from your baby's skin will make the child uncomfortably cool. Immediately after removing your baby from the tub, wrap the child securely in a towel, arms folded close to the body.

Put Safety First

Do not leave your baby alone in the tub for any reason! It only takes seconds to drown. Approximately 50 babies die each year because of this lack of foresight. Never trust an older sibling to watch the baby if you have to leave the room. Always wrap your baby in a towel and take the child with you if you must answer the phone or doorbell.

Check the water temperature with your elbow to be sure you don't scald your baby when you put the child in the tub. To prevent your baby from touching a hot faucet, run the cold water last. Keep the faucets out of your baby's reach—even tiny babies can nudge open the hot water faucet and scald themselves to death.

Do not use any plug-in electrical device in the bathroom while your baby is there.

Don't Be Upset by Your Baby's First Whimper

Whimpering at the beginning of the bath is normal and part of the process of your baby's adjustment to the change in surroundings. If you become alarmed at these first minor whimpers, your worry is transmitted to your baby, making it harder for the child to adjust to the bath's sensations. If you remain calm, gentle, and persistent, your baby is more likely to quiet.

Heed Your Baby's Reflexes

Don't assume that your baby's crying during bathtime is due to a fear of water. Bathtime crying may be reflexive, but the cause is not an inborn fear of water but more likely the Moro reflex (see chapter 3). The undressing procedure and the shaky, insecure way parents hold their baby sets off this reflex and the resulting cries. Being aware of your baby's reflexive responses and knowing how to control them is the key to enjoyable baths.

Change Your Baby's Position Often

Understimulation is devastating to your baby's physical, emotional, and intellectual development. Change the child's position in the tub, not only for comfort, but also to provide different sensations, perceptions, and to exercise different muscles.

Adjust Your Bathing Technique to Type of Tub

Sinks and dishpans: If you have a newborn, undress your baby and place the child in a semisitting position in the water, supporting the back of the head with your wrist and using the same hand to lightly grasp the child's arm farthest from you. Since most of your infant's body will be resting on the bottom of the pan, a tight hold is not necessary. Use your other hand for washing, shampooing, and rinsing.

The family tub: Whatever your baby's age, your family tub will provide the ultimate baby bath experience. For a newborn, you will have to join your baby in the tub, but for a baby who can sit up, you can either kneel at the side or get in with the child.

The water should be deep enough to cover your extended legs by at least several inches (10 to 15 cm). This depth keeps your baby warm and gives the child a chance to feel the effects of buoyancy. While getting in, hold your baby close until your child begins to relax. Then gently lay your baby on its back on your extended legs, facing you so the child retains the security of seeing your face. Later, reverse this position so that your baby's head is closest to you.

For newborns, always hold the child's arms close to the body. As you carefully wash water over your baby's body, observe how its warmth relaxes your baby. If your baby does start to cry, hug the child close to you. Make it a brief hug, though, as your baby soon will become grumpy from the cooling effects of evaporation. Breast or bottle feeding while in the tub is another way to

Gradually move the baby off your legs, supporting only his head.

calm a crying baby. After a short milk snack, your baby will be ready to begin swimming practice again.

Gradually move the baby off your legs, supporting only the upper back and head. After several swirls around the tub, allow a small amount of water to flow over your baby's face. Make sure the water flows from the top of the head toward the chin, so the direction of the water is not up the child's nose.

When you tire of swirling the child on the back, switch to a stomach position. Place your palms under your baby's chest and chin and let the water support the rest of the child's body. As you slowly swish your baby through the water, maintain eye contact while singing and talking. Continue swishing while lowering your baby's head close to the water. At first just dipping the child's chin in the water is sufficiently adventuresome, but eventually you'll be able to dip the entire face. Whenever dipping, it's crucial for the water to flow from the eyes toward the mouth, so water is not forced up the nose. Therefore, dip only when you are pulling your baby's head forward.

As your baby gets older, the child will not require as much support. In this case, the hand position with the parent's fingers passing over the baby's back and thumbs under the arms will be more comfortable for both you and your child.

After trying the back and stomach positions, move on to the sitting position. Set the baby on your thigh or between your legs, laying the child's head back against your tummy. If your baby is very young, hold the arms close to the body and offer your fingers to the child to clasp.

The end of the bath should be devoted to play. For this, the sitting position is probably most suitable. If your baby is younger than 6 months old, the child probably will be content just watching you play with toys or doing finger plays in the water.

Older babies delight in more vigorous splashing and want to play with the toys by themselves. If your baby is capable of sitting alone, the child will probably be thrilled to sit in a submerged laundry basket filled with toys. The holes in the sides of the basket provide lots of hand holds, so your baby can feel secure and independent at the same time. The child still must be watched constantly, in case he or she loses a grasp and slips underwater.

Portable plastic baby tubs: If you don't have time to get in the family tub with your baby, a portable plastic tub works well for babies older than 6 months. Its long, narrow shape allows your baby to lie back, freeing your hands so you don't have the awkward job of holding the child with one hand while washing with the other. It also lets your baby experience the feel of water in both the back and stomach positions.

Such tubs do have limitations, though. They are not deep enough for your baby to experience buoyancy, and they are not suitable for babies younger than 6 weeks or older than 1 year. Babies younger than 6 weeks need close, reassuring skin-to-skin contact with the parent, the type of contact available only when the parent gets in, too. Baby tubs are too small for that. They are also too small for babies older than a year to fully lie down.

When using a baby tub, draw water slightly warmer than desired, because such a small amount of water cools rapidly and may be too cold by the time the baby is undressed. Draw the water before undressing your baby and fill to a depth of about 3 inches (8 cm) or just enough to cover your baby's ears.

If your baby is unable to hold up the head, it's easier to bathe the child lying supine in the water. In this position, because your baby can roll the head to the side and get a mouthful of water, steady the child's head with your hand. Be careful not to touch the child's cheeks, though, and set off the rooting reflex. To prevent Moro reflexes, fold your baby's arms across the chest and hold them with the forearm of the hand you use to steady the child's head.

If your baby can hold up his or her head for at least 3 minutes, the child may enjoy lying in the stomach position and looking around. This position is great exercise for baby's back and neck muscles and, with your child's head out of the water, shampooing becomes an easy task.

Don't worry if your baby's face momentarily drops into the water. Usually the child will lift it out before inhaling. If water is inhaled, a few coughs normally take care of the situation. After one or two such instances, your baby will learn to keep the head up and to hold the breath underwater. Never force your baby to hold its head out for long periods. As soon as your child starts to tire, switch to the sitting or back position.

Baby contoured sponges and inflatable tubs: Babies cool quickly in these types of tubs as most of their body is held up out of the water. Unless the room temperature is very warm, your baby will most likely be cold and uncomfortable and learn to dislike the bath. If you do choose to use one of these devices, counteract the cooling evaporative effect of water sponged over the body by keeping the room free of drafts and very warm.

Because so little water is used, the types of water games you can play are limited. They also offer no opportunity for your baby to feel buoyancy, to learn about the physical characteristics of water through play, or to experience the basic swimming positions.

Hot Tubs

Lucky is the baby with a hot tub at home! If you have one, you can practice most of the skills taught at baby swimming lessons. But as versatile as hot tubs are, they pose special hazards. Not only can they be full of germs if not properly disinfected, but typical hot tub temperatures are too warm for your baby's comfort and can lead to serious health problems. Always use a backup thermometer as hot tub thermostats are often off by as much as 4° F (2° C). For children younger than 5 years, the water temperature must never exceed 98° F (37° C). For pregnant women, the temperature should not exceed 100° F (38° C), since temperatures over 102° F (39° C) can damage unborn fetuses in the first trimester. Unless the water is less than 95° F (35° C), don't linger in the tub more than 10 minutes to practice swimming skills.

If you would like to stay in longer, wrap your baby in a towel and set the child in an infant seat, situated so you can see your baby and the child can see you. While your baby is resting, warm and dry in the seat, you can continue soaking.

The hot tub experience will probably be pleasant for your baby and for you. The relaxed feeling it instills comes from the effect of warm water as a muscle relaxer. Your baby may like the feeling so much that the child might climb back in when you're busy in another part of the house. To prevent your child from drowning in such an instance or being scalded by overly hot water, keep the gate or door to the hot tub securely locked.

Watch out also for hot tub rash on both you and your baby. The rash is caused by a bacteria known as *pseudomonas aeruginosa*, which thrives in hot water. Onset of the rash may occur from 6 hours to 5 days after hot tub use. It may be accompanied by a low grade fever, headache, and tenderness under the arms and in the chest. Treatment is usually not necessary for any of the symptoms, and the rash normally disappears within 10 days.

This type of bacteria can be found in swimming pools as well as hot tubs. It is believed that it causes a rash more often in hot tubs than pools because the chlorine evaporates more rapidly in hot tubs, allowing the bacteria to proliferate. Physicians also suspect that the hot water itself interferes with a defense mechanism in the human body that normally protects the skin from such bacteria. To prevent *pseudomonas aeruginosa* from flourishing in your hot tub, disinfect the tub and water regularly with chlorine and check chlorine levels often.

Heart disease, diabetes, circulatory, or blood pressure ailments can all be aggravated by hot tubbing. If you or your baby has one of these conditions, check with your doctor before hopping in the tub.

References

Berman, C. (1981, June). Water babies. *Parents*, pp. 70-74.

Campbell, R. (1977). *How to really love your child*. Wheaton, IL: Scripture Press Publications.

Latta, F.F. (1949). *Handbook of Yokuts Indians*. Oildale, CA: Bear State Books.

Marks, N.J., & Mills, R.P. (1983). Swimming and grommets. *Journal of the Royal Society of Medicine*, **76**, 23-26.

Melville, H. *Typee* (pp. 241-242). New York: Dodd, Mead.

Timmermans, C. (1975). *How to teach your baby to swim*. New York: Stein & Day.

Selected Readings

Bennett, H., Wagner, T., & Fields, A. (1983). Acute hyponatremia and seizures in an infant after a swimming lesson. *Pediatrics*, **72**(1), 125-127.

Calderon, R., & Mood, E.W. (1982). An epidemiological assessment of water quality and swimmer's ear. *Archives of Environmental Health*, **37**(5), 300-305.

Chapman, D.F. (1980). Swimming and grommets. *Clinical Otolaryngology*, **5**, 420.

Clarke, D.H., & Vaccaro, P. (1979). The effect of swimming training on muscular performance and body composition in children. *Research Quarterly*, **50**(1), 9-17.

David, R., Ellis, P., & Gaitner, J.C. (1981). Water intoxication in normal infants: Role of antidiuretic hormone in pathogenesis. *Pediatrics*, **68**, 349-353.

Diem, L. *Report of a longitudinal study about the effects of early motor stimulation on the development of personality of the child from 4-6 years.* Unpublished manuscript. (Available from Blumenaller 24, 5000 Cologne, Federal Republic of Germany)

Elsner, R., & Gooden, B. (1983). Diving and asphyxia. Cambridge, MA: Cambridge University Press. *Monographs of the Physiological Society*, **40**, 1-168.

Feinmesser, R., Wiesel, Y.M., Argaman, M., & Gay, I. (1982). Otitis externa—bacteriological survey. *ORL: Journal of Otorhinolaryngology*, **44**(3), 121-125.

Galbraith, N.S. (1980). Infections associated with swimming pools. *Environmental Health*, **88**, 31-33.

Goldberg, G.N., Lightner, E.S., & Morgan, W. (1982). Infantile water intoxication after a swimming lesson. *Pediatrics*, **70**(4), 599-600.

Haag, J.R., & Gieser, R.G. (1983). Effects of swimming pool water on the cornea. *JAMA: Journal of the American Medical Association*, **249**(18), 2507-2508.

Hoadley, A.W., & Knight, D.E. (1975). External otitis among swimmers and non-swimmers. *Archives of Environmental Health*, **30**, 445-448.

Malina, R.M. (1983). Human growth, maturation, and regular physical activity. *Acta Medica Auxologica*, **15**(1), 5-27.

Mayerhoffer, A.A. (1952). *Swimming movements in infants*. Unpublished doctoral dissertation, Leipzig University, East Germany. (Translated from the German by A. Tegen, 1974)

McGraw, M.B. (1939). Swimming behavior of the human infant. *Journal of Pediatrics*, **15**, 485-490.

Morrison, H. (1956). Jungle journeys in Sarawak. *The National Geographic Magazine*, **109**(5), 710-736.

Newman, V.H. (1967). *Teaching an infant to swim*. New York: Harcourt, Brace & World.

Schiefflin, J.W. (1977). A new technique of water survival training for infants and toddlers. *Pediatric Annals*, **6**(11), 45-50.

Smelt, G.J., & Yeoh, L.H. (1984). Swimming and grommets. *Journal of Laryngology and Otology*, **98**(3), 243-245.

VanDyk, D. (1975). Water safety for infants: The drownproofing method. Melbourne: Lansdowne Press.

White, B. (1980). *A parent's guide to the first three years*. Englewood Cliffs, NJ: Prentice Hall.

Wright, D.N., & Alexander, J.M. (1974). Effect of water on the bacterial flora of swimmers ears. *Archives of Otolaryngology*, **95**, 15-18.

Index